Foot Solutions, a proud advocate & supporter of
Susan G. Komen for the Cure®,
introduces Pink Pole Balance Walking,
a program to help you enjoy a low impact complete
program to help change your life and create a new you.

From October 1, 2009 through December 31, 2011,
FOOT SOLUTIONS will donate $2 for every book and
$5 for every set of PINK POLES sold to Susan G. Komen
for the Cure® with a minimum guaranteed donation of
$100,000.

Pink Pole Balance Walking

Copyright © 2008-2010 by Ray Margiano

All rights reserved. No part of this book may be reproduced or transmitted in any form or by any means without written permission of the author.

ISBN 978-0-615-34561-1

Cover

Stephanie Herbst Lucke – mother, master runner and motivator

Katie Ingraham – Blogger and trainer

Photo by Phil Parker

Dedication

I would like to dedicate this book to Susan G. Komen for the Cure® and everyone associated with the organization; from the excellent, passionate corporate staff to all the Affiliates and walkers supporting the program. To any of you readers who have been impacted in any way by breast cancer, and especially every survivor who has taken a stand to fight and live their life, this book is for you and written in your honor.

Amanda

Great meeting you and hope to get a chance to work with you

Ray [illegible]

Special Dedication

Thank you, mom, for being the wonderful person that you were and for helping me become who I am.

Neda Marazzi Margiano

To my mom who died of cancer in 1996 – this is a devastating disease that we must challenge and conquer. I couldn't help mom but maybe I can help you.

To My Readers

Family and friends are so important in life. Never miss an opportunity.

If you have picked this book up and thumbed through its pages, I request just one thing. Give yourself 15 minutes each day for 3 months using this system of balance. If you don't feel more alive, more energetic, younger, and if your friends and family have not noticed a difference in you; then please Email me and I will have one of our coaches personally contact you to review what you are doing and how we can help you. This book is based on simple lifestyle changes that can have a very profound impact on you.

Time is the one thing we cannot control and the one thing we never have enough of. In today's complex world, it is worse than ever before. Most of us rush through our days and have nothing left for ourselves.

This system started out as a program to help me change my lifestyle, to reduce my stress levels, to lose weight, to increase my energy level and to take my life back. I know it works, not only from my own personal results, but from the hundreds of coaches and advocates we have worked with; from the countless hugs and thank you notes received including from people who have very serious issues and medical challenges to deal with.

Once this book helps you change your lifestyle and/or helps you achieve a new sense of balance in your life that is important to you, I will be humbled and honored to have shared this system with you. Remember, this is all about you. It represents simple lifestyle changes that can help you live a fuller, healthier, happier life and help you refocus on what is important to you. In short, these are simple steps to achieving the objectives you set for yourself. If you commit to this system, you will succeed!

In fact, I promise you results if you try the Pink Pole Balance Walking program for just thirty days.

Thirty days are just what you need to whet your appetite. We want this to be your lifestyle change. If you do not see or notice a change in yourself, please Email me at ceo@footsolutions.com and one of our coaches will directly advise you and help you get on track. If you still don't see or feel a difference, I will personally refund to you the cost of this book.

Acknowledgements

I wish to acknowledge a number of people whose help and contributions made this book possible.

To all members of my family who have accepted me and my workaholic pace and lifestyle, thank you.

Every book is built on input and contributions developed over time. For everyone who has helped and contributed to my journey through life and experience, thank you.

Special thanks to Susan G. Komen for the Cure®. Everyone I worked with or talked to in the organization has been extremely co-operative and supportive. Thanks go out to Ira Blumenthal, author and business consultant for his endless suggestions, reviews, comments and input as well as to Terry Kennedy, Head Coach and Mentor for the Balance Walking and mentoring network.

Special thanks also to Kimberly Hard, Founder & CEO of 'Be Well Atlanta' and Coach Sue Bozgoz for her tireless support and input when I first launched Balance Walking. I also thank Donna Robertson, Sports Pedorthist specialist, Dr. William Faddock DPM, C.Ped, Dr. Craig Aaron, Chiropractor, author and yoga specialist, Teresa Tapp, author of Fit and Fabulous in 15 minutes and creator of T-Tapp and my assistant Alison Strohfus for the many retypes and editing suggestions.

I also thank my many international coaches and affiliates from Europe who are very involved in pole walking and documenting the positive results. A special thank you to Dr. Klaus Schwanbeck, German pole walking expert and Olympic trainer who also trained me on the European approach to pole walking (the author of The Ultimate Nordic Pole Walking Book). Thanks also to Michael Ertl, President and Founder of Chung Shi, Germany. Finally thank you to all the wonderful people I have met and discussed Balance Walking with around the world, especially in Italy, Finland and Holland.

Notice

This book is intended as a reference, overview and introduction only. The information presented is not a medical manual and this information is not a substitute for any treatment that may have been prescribed by your doctor. If you think you have medical issues or problems you should always see a doctor.

All rights reserved. No part of this publication may be reproduced or transmitted in any form or by any means without the written permission of the author.

Understand that you are solely responsible for the way this information is perceived and utilized and do so at your own risk. In no way will the author be responsible for injuries or other problems that might occur due to the use of this material or any actions taken based on the content of this material. The author will not be held responsible for the conduct of any companies and websites recommended within this book.

Mention of companies, organizations or authorities does not imply that they have endorsed this book or the author.

Now that we have gotten this out of the way let's get out there and live life to the fullest... to its balanced fullest!

Table of Contents

Everyone needs to climb to the top of their mountain
no matter how small or how high.
We are only limited by our own imaginations.

Author & Founder of the Balance Walking concept
Ray Margiano, PhD

THE PINK POLE BALANCE WALKING WAY OF LIFE

This is a complete health and wellness program that covers the 4 pillars necessary to achieve a well balanced lifestyle for you.

1. Low Impact Activity

This is the major cornerstone of the Balance Walking Program. The technique is based on Balance Pole Walking that will help you increase the calorie burn rate in less time. You will engage 90% your core muscle groups while aligning your body for improved posture and body function. You will burn up to 50% more calories than regular walking.

2. Stress Reduction

Stress, along with being a contributor to your belt size, is also a factor in many other health issues, including obesity, heart disease and breast cancer. Since the goal of Balance Walking is for you to become healthier and more active, stress reduction is an important cornerstone of the program. This simple approach will rejuvenate your mind and body.

3. Food for Life

Throw diets out! They just do not work long-term. Eating is a joy of life that should be enjoyed. By eating less processed and more natural foods, as well as eating smaller portions more often, eating can be both enjoyable and healthy. You'll stop counting calories and worrying about what you can't eat, and will be more satisfied. Eat, drink and be merry – life is simple, why do we complicate it?

4. Toning

Maintaining and toning muscles will keep you looking younger and more active. Balance Walking includes some simple non time-consuming ways to maintain and tone your body, which will also kick start your metabolism rate! The average person loses approximately 30% of their muscle mass between the ages of 20 – 70.

The 'Pink Pole Balance Walking Movement' is a "fit for life" program that involves simple changes that anyone can do quickly and easily and will help you adjust to a lifestyle that is right for a healthier, more active you. It only requires as little as 15 minutes per day.

You will feel energized, relaxed, look and act years younger with no pills, no excuses and you can do this now!

A Low-Impact Activity for Everyone. Busy Lifestyles - No time, no energy - A great simple solution

INTRODUCTION

Daily exercise, one of the essential components for good health, is fun and easy with Pink Pole Balance Walking. Simply stated, Pink Pole Balance Walking increases your benefits in reduced time. Time is the key factor that will impact whatever you pursue, which is why it is so critical to choose some form of activity you can do anywhere, anytime, and easily blend it into your lifestyle.

In addition, you want a complete program that is simple and very inexpensive that you can do alone, with family, friends or support groups.

TIME

Time is the one thing none of us have enough of!

Typically when reviewing a fitness program, everyone wants to know...

- How long will it take?
- How much time does it require each day?
- How much weight can I lose?
- How much time must I dedicate to Balance Walking?
- How much time will I need to learn how to Balance Walk?
- How long will it take to get back in shape?

There is a very simple answer to all of these questions. "It will take the rest of your life!" Pink Pole Balance Walking is a life long process which you'll need to practice with a simple investment of just 15 minutes a day, every day.

The results will enrich the quality of your life. Our bodies are constantly changing and adjusting through all stages of a lifetime and life cycle.

A simple question to ask yourself everyday, "Where are you going?"

Then ask yourself, "Why?"

Why is quiet time or meditation so important at this stage in your life?

- First, it will give you a sense of peace.
- A sense of oneness with life and all of those in your life.
- A sense of strength to face whatever consequence that will come to you.

LIVE EACH DAY

Sometimes just a few moments makes a big difference in both of your lives.

As my colleague Ira Blumenthal says "We are activity rich and time poor."

Reach out to someone you love today and every day for the rest of your life!

Walking

Did you know that the average person walks the equivalent distance of 3.5 times around the world during their lifetime?

Walking is the world's oldest and most popular form of exercise, with the least amount of strain on the body. In the U.S., it is estimated that there are approximately 90 million walkers.

Unfortunately, most people do not receive the full potential benefits from their walks, and see little improvement over time. In addition, most people think walking is boring and too time-consuming (with little fitness results).

If you can walk, you can do this.

Well, friends, traditional walking has just been given a shot of adrenaline - Pink Pole Balance Walking allows you to accomplish much more in less time. Through the combination of today's technology and years of accumulated knowledge on walking techniques, we have created Pink Pole Balance Walking. It is more fun, requires less time, and with the simple addition of two components, walking poles and a specially designed Balance Walking shoe, your benefits from the program will increase.

With the Pink Pole Balance Walking System, you get more of a workout for every fitness level, with less time. You'll work up to 90% of your muscles while you walk using the Pink Pole Balance Walking System. Although you are using more muscles, there is no unusual strain on the body and it will feel completely natural. In addition to increased muscle use and activation, you will be able to increase your calorie burn rate up to 50% more than through regular walking. This means that people with time constraints can get sufficient results in less time.

Balance Walking gives you an upper-body workout while you walk. It builds arm, shoulder and back muscles while reducing tension in your shoulders, neck and back. It also gets your heart pumping, thus allowing you to reach your target heart-rate without the negative impact that running or other strenuous forms of pounding exercise have on your body. This means more calorie burn and improved cardiovascular performance while using up to 90% of your muscles.

Although Balance Walking can be done with any comfortable walking or running shoe, our Balance Walking specialty shoes are uniquely designed to increase the benefits of Balance Walking by working your core muscles, toning and strengthening your abs, muscles, buttocks and back. They force better posture and target under-utilized muscles, building more muscle mass and in turn increasing calorie consumption. They may also improve or reduce varicose veins and the appearance of cellulite and ultimately help stomp out fat. They will also improve and strengthen your core and pelvic floor muscles.

The components that make up this breakthrough in exercise have been thoroughly tested and validated, providing much documentation and studies to support the individual components of Pink Pole Balance Walking and its benefits.

Pink Pole Balance Walking has been created to bring basic, fundamental, well-proven concepts together to introduce you to a lifestyle change you can enjoy and easily accomplish for the rest of your life.

Again, devote a minimum of 15 minutes a day to Pink Pole Balance Walking and you and your friends will notice the difference. Better yet, include your friends and family in this very beneficial way of life. It is child friendly and we have successfully implemented these programs in retirement communities, in schools, for athletes etc. Make this a special time to bond and share quality time with others. You can also spend quiet time alone with this program. There is nothing more stress relieving than a quiet walk by your self.

Foundations of a Successful Fitness Program

Look and feel better.

- ✓ Don't wait for a new year to make your resolution to get back into shape and to eat better. DO IT NOW.
- ✓ If you are undergoing any medical therapy, issues or medication or have any issues or concerns, make sure you check with your healthcare professionals to consider any special concerns that should be considered before starting your program.
- ✓ Setting specific objectives that are reasonable will help you achieve results.

Note: you are not going to lose all the weight you gained in the last 5 years in the next 5 weeks. The body responds quickly but not that quickly.

Identify where you are today:

- Weight	- Strength
- Flexibility	- Endurance

This allows you to measure and plot progress.

Create a support system:

Find a coach or mentor in your area for Balance Walking.

Do it daily – only 15 minutes!

Can't find one or don't want one?

Then visit www.balancewalking.com and work with an online buddy, or compete against yourself.

Treat yourself.

Accomplish some of your goals – reward yourself with some new gear or a full body massage.

NO MORE EXCUSES

You will meet great people.

1. I AM NOT INTO EXERCISING!

Pink Pole Balance Walking is low impact, easy to do and less stressful than most exercising, with up to a 50% more calorie burn than regular walking. Yet, something as simple as walking is actually easier because the poles give you a better sense of balance and support.

2. I DON'T HAVE TIME!

Time and convenience is probably the biggest challenge for most people. With only 15 minutes per day, the Pink Pole Balance Walking Program is designed to give you more benefits in less time using proven concepts, plus you can do it any time and any place. This requires no drive to the gym, no shower needed after your walk and no fuss, no bother. Oh I said a no, no! Simply put, this is a casual 15 to 20 minute Balance Walk which will not leave you sweaty and in need of a shower and a clothing change.

3. EXERCISE IS BORING AND I AM NOT COORDINATED!

Pink Pole Balance Walking is a combination of simple, efficient, proven concepts that offer you an easy way to change your lifestyle. The primary concept is based on pole walking, simple stress reduction sessions, flexibility, basic muscle toning/shaping and healthy eating habits. You can do this alone or as a social activity with a group, trainer, family or friends. If you can walk you can do this. I don't care what kind of shape you are in – this will help you!

4. CAN'T GET TO THE GYM!

Balance Walking can be done anywhere, anytime and is very inexpensive. Check www.balancewalking.com for group walks or coaches in your area, and network with people just like you. So what's your excuse now?

Any place, any time !

GET BACK IN THE GAME

- With Balance Walking, it is all about you.
- For just 15 minutes a day, it is just you. Give yourself 15 minutes every day!
- You can fulfill your own potential.

- How far and how long you go is up to you. Sometimes you may want to change up your speed just for the extra shot in the arm. Again, it's always your choice.
- How fast you go is up to you.
- No one is chasing you; it is your body and your mind. Get 50% more benefits over regular walking without feeling additional exertion, plus! If you want to push the envelope. Most of us will be fine with just a normal pace.

Balance Walking can be your fountain of youth.

If you want to drink from the fountain of youth, if you want to help your body fight off disease, if you want to find an inner peace, if you are interested in anti-aging benefits and a slew of things you will feel better about, then make this 15 minute commitment and live a fuller, more active, more balanced life.

Reduce the time and impact to your body – switch to Balance Walking.

The Chinese have a saying that 10,000 steps per day lead to a healthy mind and healthy body. Through the use of Pink Pole Balance Walking system and specially designed Balance Walking shoes you can reduce this number down to 5,000 steps per day and get similar benefits. This is a 50% savings in time; the one element that impacts most people and most programs and the one thing no one has enough of.

1. Dr. Cedric Bryant, Chief Science Officer for The American Council on Exercise (ACE) states "It's so low impact and joint friendly, and it's a relatively simple way of taking what many people are already doing, walking, and boosting it up a notch to burn extra calories." – The Wall Street Journal, 2/1/07.

2. "As a trainer and athlete, I am amazed with Balance Walking. Regardless of your age, you can walk to good health. You use 90% of your muscles, it is low-impact and you can have fun while exercising. I have clients with Parkinson's and other medical conditions who have difficulty walking. With the Balance Walking poles they are now walking with better posture and able to work out with more intensity. I have another client who has lost 12 pounds in 6 weeks of Balance Walking. I can't say enough!" – Karen J. Iverson RN, CPT, CFT, Fitness Practitioner, CHN, Balance Walking Master Instructor.

3. Cooper Institute Study Summary, September, 2002, validates increased calorie burn as well as no perceived increase in exertion.

   The Cooper Institute in Texas compared physiological responses of pole walking to regular walking. The calorie expenditure and the oxygen consumption increased an average of 20%, and the heart-rate increased with 10 beats per minute when using the walking poles. The interesting thing is that even though the body works harder using the poles, the RPE (rated perceived exertion) was the same walking with or without poles.

   Dr. Tim Church said, "Some individuals increased as much as 46% in oxygen consumption and just about the same in calorie expenditure."

Quotes from study:

✓ "Individuals who poled more intensely had higher oxygen consumption."

✓ "There is potential for considerably more or less benefit depending on the selection of poling-off intensity. This may have particular significance for individuals who need to increase calorie expenditure but have walking speed limitations."

- ✓ "Increased calorie expenditure, with no corresponding increase in perceived exertion during pole walking, may have important public health applications."

The Effects of Walking Poles on Shoulder Function in Breast Cancer Survivors

Study completed by Lisa K. Sprod, MS, Scott N. Drum, MS, Ann T. Bentz, PhD, Susan D. Carter, MD, Carole M. Schneider, PhD & Carole M. Schneider, PhD - University of Northern Colorado, Rocky Mountain Cancer Rehabilitation Institute, Greeley, Colorado. Integrative Cancer Therapies, Dec 2005; vol 4: pp.287 – 293.

Breast cancer treatment often results in impaired shoulder function, in particular, decrements in muscular endurance and range of motion, which may lead to decreased quality of life. The purpose of this investigation was to determine the effects of walking pole use on shoulder function in female breast cancer survivors. Participants had previously been treated with one or a combination of the following: mastectomy, breast conservation therapy, axillary lymph node dissection, chemotherapy, or radiation.

Participants were randomly placed in experimental and control groups and met with a cancer exercise specialist 2 times each week for 8 weeks. The experimental group used walking poles during the 20-minute aerobic portion of their workout, whereas the control group did not use pole walking but performed 20 minutes of aerobic exercise per workout session. Both groups participated in similar resistance training programs. Testing was done pre- and post-exercise intervention to determine upper body muscular endurance and active range of motion at the glenohumeral joint.

Repeated-measures analysis of variance revealed significant improvements in muscular endurance as measured by the bench press and lat pull down in the pole walking group. No within-group improvements were found in the group that did not use walking poles.

The data suggest that using a walking pole exercise routine for 8 weeks significantly improved muscular endurance of the upper body, which would clearly be beneficial in helping breast cancer survivors perform activities of daily living and regain an independent lifestyle.

Breast Cancer and Pole Walking

German Cancer Study

Study done in Germany on pole walking and breast cancer by Dr. Freerk T. Baumann (Institute for Rehabilitation and Sports for the Handicapped at German Sport University of Cologne).

Many women are still insecure about exercising and breast cancer. Many patients ask themselves, is this sport or movement making things even worse for me, can it cause lymphedema?

Recent studies continue to reinforce the positive affects exercising has on the breast cancer patient medically, physically, mentally and overall attitude and quality of life.

New scientific studies show that pole walking done properly has a positive effect on the body. Pink Pole Balance Walking improves your stamina and endurance as well as your overall body fitness. At the same time, you improve circulation in your shoulders and arms. In addition, your back and neck muscles become stronger and the neck muscles relax. The poles are a very good motivation and help secure your balance.

Study by Donna Robertson, Athletic Trainer and C.Ped

Over the years I have worked with a number of breast cancer patients. With my recent studies and cases I have introduced the concept of Balance Walking using the rocker bottom Chung Shi shoe. My case study findings have included increased and improved range of motion for the mastectomy patients; in addition I have noted improvement to postural balance and muscle tone. The actual use of the Balance Walking poles helps with lymphatic drainage.

Most patients show decreased stress on their muscles in the shoulder and upper back area as well as the lower back and leg muscles. This aides greatly in stability and range of motion especially for the recovering patient.

When you are ready to exercise, Balance Walking will definitely help to get rid of your fears and insecurities. The best thing to do is become a member of a Balance Walking Group where you will get free training, and it is much more fun to exercise in a group. With Balance Walking there are special rules for breast cancer patients that should be followed.

Rules before beginning (following surgery)

You should start, at the earliest, 2 months after your breast operation and make sure you check with your doctor before starting the program. The surgical wounds must be fully healed. To prevent the risk of lymphedema you can wear elastic stockings on your arms. Now you are ready to start with the program. In the beginning the rule is do not over exert yourself, start with 10 minutes to increase your body stamina. Before you start, begin with a short warm up!

Great to do with a friend.

Warm Up:

1. Walk a couple of minutes without the poles and shake your arms lightly.

2. Put your arms in the air, and box with your hands in a fist towards the sky about 15-20 seconds, let the arms drop after that and make an active walking movement with your arms backwards and forwards for about a minute.

3. Stretch your arms again to the sky, open, and close your hands when your arms are in the air. With this you activate the muscle pump and you're preventing a lymphedema (15-20 seconds).

Note: The movement of Balance Walking is very helpful in exercising chest, shoulders, arms and back muscles. In addition, the release and hand grip action further aides in the flow of blood and pump action in the arms and shoulders which aide in preventing lymphedema.

The correct movement training:

You can review basic procedures on how to pole walk using Balance Walking proper techniques in this book or visit www.balancewalking.com for video of basic instructions. Or better yet, find a Balance Walking coach near you or a Foot Solutions store location for free introductory lessons.

If you are recovering from surgery or undergoing treatment, you should stop or not practice Balance Walking under the following conditions:

- Metastasis
- Abrupt bleedings
- Thrombosis
- Heavy pains
- Fainting
- State of confusion
- Light headed
- Temperature
- Infections
- Upset stomach
- Osteoporosis
- Heart problems

Start slowly at first: only 10 minutes 3 times a week depending on your condition and shape. Over several weeks, work at a pace comfortable for you; work yourself up to 15 minutes a day of Pink Pole Balance Walking. Rest whenever you need to and also skip a day or two anytime you need to.

The Breast Cancer Survivor's Fitness Plan

From the experts at Harvard Medical School - Carolyn M. Kaelin, M.D., M.P.H.

Sarcopenia – simultaneous loss of muscle and rise in fat tissue.

Key health concerns due to treatment including surgery, radiation, and/or anti-cancer drugs all will slow you down or make it much more difficult for you to accomplish your objectives.

- Added weight
- Dwindling muscles
- Loss of bone mass

Why is healthy weight so important?

- ✓ Research indicates avoiding weight gain or losing weight if you are already overweight can cut recurrence rate and may improve survival.
- ✓ Reducing risk of lymphedema. Yes, there is an increased risk if you are overweight.
- ✓ Want to outlive breast cancer? Then take the weight off so you can reduce the odds of many other ailments that are tied directly to weight gain.
- ✓ Reducing the risk of lymphedema – new thinking suggests that gradual, progressive training like Balance Walking may actually minimize the chances of developing lymphedema by helping dilate remaining lymphatic channels in the shoulder and underarm areas.
- ✓ Recovering from surgery – to recover as fully as possible you need to regain posture, improve balance, flexibility and strength. Pink Pole Balance Walking is a natural for this.
- ✓ The great thing about Pink Pole Balance Walking is it includes the right mix of elements and exercises to take on each area of concern and those major areas identified in numerous studies. It is a full program, even covering stress release approaches as well as the basic pole walking portion that will help you exercise shoulder, chest, back – full body – 90% of your muscles in a very controlled low impact way and a calorie burn rate of up to 50% over regular walking.

Join our blog: www.balancewalking.com. Let us help advise and council you. We will openly respond to all questions and also help you join a group that is right for you.

The 4 Pillars of Pink Pole Balance Walking

Balance Walking combines the 4 pillars of health with complimentary elements that produce a synergistic effect unlike any other single program of its kind. It is the blend of activities and disciplines that will help restore and rejuvenate your life and energy; *all in just 15 minutes a day.*

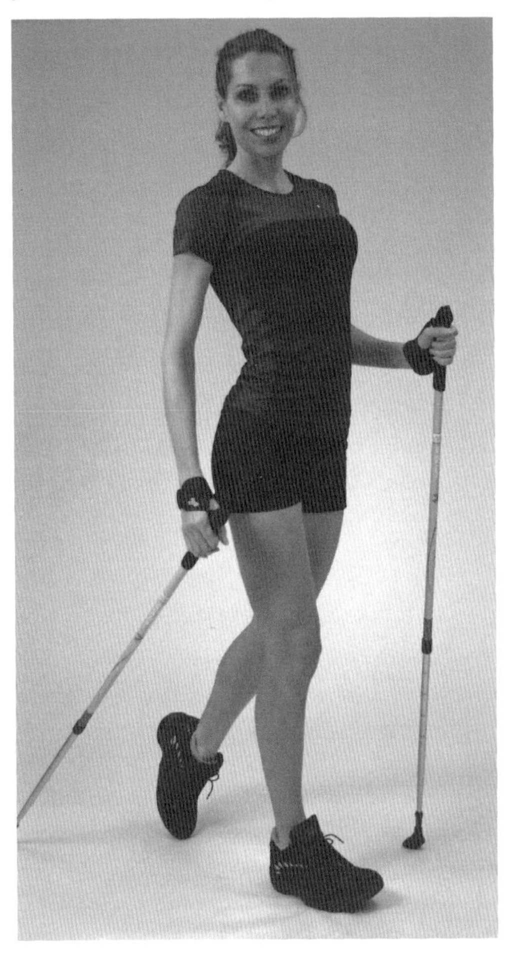

Pink Pole Balance Walking is about changing the way you live simply and easily to help guide you into a more healthful and balanced lifestyle. Achieving physical fitness alone is not the solution.

The formulation for a balanced lifestyle includes:

1. Low Impact Activity
2. Stress Reduction
3. Food for Life (no dieting)
4. Toning/Flexibility

Pink Pole Balance Walking provides a full foundation from which to face the day to day stresses of life, not only for survival purposes, but also to help you lead a very active full life for the rest of your life.

Stress alone has more of an impact on your body and state of health than any other function. At the heart of this holistic approach to taking care of you is finding that quiet safe place you can go to any time you want to.

Sometimes the simplest pleasures are best.

Some of the Benefits of Pink Pole Balance Walking:

- Helps you look and feel years younger
- Burns up to 50% more calories than traditional walking
- Strengthens core muscles – tones abs, buttocks, and back muscles
- Reduces stress to knees, hips and back up to 30%
- Increases strength and endurance
- Enhances cardiovascular performance up to 22%
- Improves posture and body alignment
- Relieves pain and tension in neck, shoulders and back
- Connects mind, body & spirit, promoting a positive healthy lifestyle
- Increases circulation in feet and legs
- Improves respiration
- Improves pelvic floor muscles
- Activates foot reflexology zones
- May improve or reduce varicose veins
- Reduces appearance of cellulite
- Improves balance and performance
- Reduces weight
- Reduces tension
- Improves overall health and fitness

Don't we all want to look and feel good?

Turning back the Clock with Pink Pole Balance Walking

Do you have these symptoms?

- Hot flashes
- Low libido
- Increased skin wrinkling
- Irregular periods
- Insomnia
- Mood swings
- Fatigue
- Slow weight loss

Then Balance Walking is one answer for you!

Isn't it time to live your life?

Don't you want these feelings?

- Increased energy
- Improved muscle tone
- Decreased body fat
- Better sleep
- Increased libido
- Sharper thinking

Make a 15 minute a day commitment.

Keep a daily log of:

- What you eat
- Your physical activity
- How you feel
- And track weight progress (if that is an issue for you)

Activity Goal

Commit to just 15 minutes per day of physical activity based on your current level of fitness, needs and objectives.

Are you in...

- Preventative mode?
- Building body strength and immune system?
- Building endurance for a 3 day walk?
- In treatment?
- In recovery?
- Raising the bar on your life?

There is a program to fit your needs and wants.

Group walking is fun, too.

Making Change Work in Your Life

Simple - your mind and body needs consistency over time to establish or to break a habit.

Note: Your mind does not know if it is a good or bad habit you are establishing.

How to start – identify and list those habits you want to change or establish.

Some of the habits that are difficult to part with...

- ⃠ Smoking
- ⃠ Drinking
- ⃠ TV
- ⃠ Caffeine
- ⃠ Texting – especially while driving
- ⃠ Eating too much or the wrong foods

I am sure you have something you want to add to the list.

Remember, anything to excess is bad!

Retrain your brain

- Make small adjustments
- Keep track daily
- Repeat good habits and alternative positive change over and over

This will set you in motion for every habit you want to add or eliminate.

If for some reason you have a bad day, week or month you can always start over. I have personally found that keeping a daily journal on what I eat and exercise for the day helps me stay focused and also allows me to adjust in a very timely fashion. To keep the habit in place you have to pay attention to drift and catch it before you are too far off course.

The Secret to Staying Motivated

Part of our Pink Pole Balance Walking Plan is to help you stay motivated. The secret to staying motivated is to form a realistic physical fitness goal. For example, committing to Balance Walking 15 minutes per day, everyday is achievable and realistic. Each day after your activity, keep track by logging your minutes into your personal log or one of our many affiliate walking programs. Check out our website for current programs and options. (www.balancewalking.com)

We have found that getting involved with other members in your area or even friends in another part of the country is a great way to chart progress and create excitement and camaraderie among Balance Walking groups and each other.

Balance Walking groups can also compete against each other or as teams; check the Balance Walking website for a Balance Walking coach or group in your area and for free introductory classes located near you. Attending group walks and events will improve your form and help keep you motivated to accomplish your personal goals.

Better yet, start or join a Balance Walking group in your area. This is a very simple process and a great way to promote Balance Walking in your area; start one now in your neighborhood, club, church, work etc.

Help lower your risk, your family's, and your friends' in just minutes a day with this very simple and convenient program. Visit www.balancewalking.com for more information.

Social Events/Race Walks
Participate in causes, they will energize you.
Organized Balance Walking for great causes,
and of course the biggest cause is you!

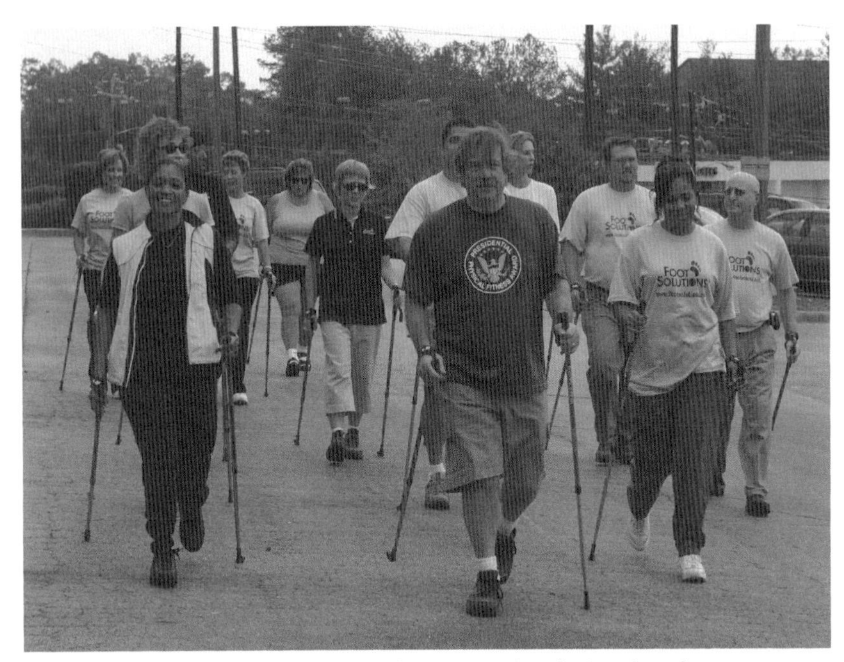

Work is no excuse – take an easy lunch time break.

Walk before work, walk on your coffee break, walk at the end of the work day while traffic is still a killer.

Join others across the world as they pledge to start a healthier BALANCED lifestyle. Make a commitment today – just 15 minutes every day!

Pink Pole Balance Walking is about creating balance in your life, with some basic lifestyle changes that are easy to adapt to:

- Making you look years younger
- Produce a feeling of well being
- Feeling of being fit
- Better health
- Increase strength
- Tone body and muscles

A Low-Impact Activity for Everyone

Busy Lifestyles - Great Solution

Daily exercise, an essential component for good health, is fun and easy with Pink Pole Balance Walks - double your benefits in just half the time.

More Benefits Than You Would Expect.

Research and studies document the results. Thousands of individuals have made positive improvements in:

- Osteoporosis
- Obesity
- Diabetes
- Fibromyalgia
- Arthritis
- Pre- and post-natal care
- Surgery recovery
- Athletic training
- Depression
- And much more!

Fitness Trend for the New Millennium

Change up your walking locations for extra boost.

Balance Walking – the activity for anyone, anywhere, at any age, with any lifestyle. Pink Pole Balance Walking is inexpensive. Learn how now and walk with our well-established network of coaches and classes.

Anyone Can Do This:

Age is not a barrier. The poles improve balance and stability making you more confident, as you continue to strengthen and tone. Feel fit and fabulous while you walk. Many users consider Balance Walking as the fountain of youth. We've all been searching for it; I have seen so many changes and improvements in individuals and even in myself. I don't know of any better feeling than the one you get from helping someone else.

Children love Balance Walking, too:

They can walk, run, jump and train simply and safely, making this sporting activity a family affair that can bridge the generation gap.

Walking for most kids is just plain boring (for most adults too).

The poles add a new dimension, now there is a new excitement and something to do with their hands, arms and bodies.

You can easily make this a family event.

Do it together as a family.

What are people saying about Balance Walking

Pink Pole Walking, a Fitness Trend for Walkers of All Ages, Sizes and Fitness Levels

Balance Walking is fast becoming a year-round, worldwide fitness trend. You are part of that trend and part of making history for your fitness and for our partnership with Susan G. Komen for the Cure®. While the virtues of using poles are well known among those who hit the ski slopes, Balance Walking Poles are quickly making their way to walking and hiking trails, neighborhoods, beaches, tracks, and even shopping malls.

We now play a major role at fund raising events and many marathons. Our goal is to get over 1 million walkers into the Pink Pole Walking Program in a three year plan. This is not only to help raise funds for Susan G. Komen for the Cure®, but more importantly to provide a program on health and wellness to millions of women to get active and to help themselves.

Dr. Art Lee, a heart surgeon at Grady Hospital in Atlanta, Georgia, adds, "Balance Walking provides a low impact and joint friendly mechanism for my patients. Post-surgery individuals, many of whom are older or obese, benefit from physical activity, and Balance Walking is a perfect tool to get these people moving safely and efficiently. It's also a stress and tension reducer, which is important to recovery."

"My lifestyle is busy, and my body was unfortunately showing signs of inactivity and weight gain. My lower back was making it difficult to enjoy my students and family. I joined the Walk Club at school with my faculty friends and within the first 2 weeks my back pain WAS GONE and I had already lost 4 pounds." -Robin T. – 2nd Grade Teacher & Mom

"As a 60-year-old active physician, it was immediately obvious the value of pole walking. Many of my patients were stuck in a rut of needing to exercise but not feeling comfortable in traditional gyms or training regimens. Balance Walking is the best low-impact, cardio activity I have come across. Our patients walk for their heart, their health and their life." -Dr. Art L. – Heart Surgeon Inner City Hospital

"Our neighborhood Balance Walking class has gotten the whole family outdoors together at least 3 times per week. We have significantly impacted our insulin dependence, improved family dynamics and feel great. There is even a high school program to get the teenagers on their feet whether they are track stars or in the marching band." -Michael, Michelle & Laura D. – A diabetic family

"Our busy practice has totally benefited from our Balance Walking Classes. We have pregnant moms, mature patients and staff, all walking, sharing ideas and staying fit. It's a win-win for women's health!" -Nurse Denise M & Dr. Carol H – OB/GYN

"I'm a certified coach, retired U.S. Army Lieutenant Colonel, war vet, motivational speaker, an All-Army marathoner and track runner. I've run; I've coached; I've trained. Never before, have I encountered an activity that is perfect for elite athletes as a recovery and training tool and, at the same time, perfect for the majority of our population." -Coach Sue B- a USATF, RRCA and Balance Walking Master instructor

"I was first introduced to Balance Walking through my sister Michele, while living in Europe. Balance Walking was simply a part of her daily workout regimen. Never one to be left behind, I got a pair of Chung Shi shoes and started using Balance Walking as a cross training tool.

"Balance Walking has been a strategic training tool for me. It has not only increased my balance, posture and overall core by stretching out my calf muscles, it has helped me avoid chronic training injuries like plantar fasciitis and Achilles tendonitis. It is simply the equivalent of a cardio workout and Pilates combined."
-Stephanie Herbst Lucke, mother, runner and motivator.

"Why I was drawn to Balance Walking!

The word 'balance' comes up in my life consistently. Enough that I'm finally paying attention. Fifteen years ago when I was setting up my company, I called it Balance For Health. I don't even know why. It just came to me and felt right so I went with it.

That name has proven to be a blueprint for my business. We don't have optimal health when our lives and bodies aren't in balance. It's the balance between the yin and the yang. The masculine and the feminine. Working and playing. Activity and rest. Taking care of everyone else and taking care of ourselves.

When I was presented with the opportunity to share a new way of life called Balance Walking, I was instantly intrigued. I had studied many different walking techniques and had done Nordic

Walking and Exerstriding for years. What made me excited about Balance Walking was its emphasis on the lifestyle associated with it.

Balance Walking is a program for everyone. Even if you've never 'exercised', you can use the walking poles with this simple technique and feel the positive difference it makes in your health and in your life."

Renee McLaughlin, Certified Health Coach - Take Shape For Life, ACE-Certified Lifestyle & Weight Management, Sr. Certified T-Tapp Trainer, Master Balance Walking Coach.

A number of elite runners are now using the Balance Walking program as a low impact recovery method.

CHAPTER 1

LOW IMPACT ACTIVITY

Balance Walking – This is the cornerstone.

The Advantages of Pole Walking

- ✓ Pole walking can be learned very easily and fast because it is a natural form of movement.
- ✓ Pole walking provides a secure feeling while walking on uneven ground and represents a more secure walking option for elderly people.
- ✓ Pole walking can be performed throughout the year anywhere.
- ✓ Pole walking can also be performed in your neighborhood, at the park, the mall, etc. The poles are collapsible and travel very easily.
- ✓ The increased fat burning, strengthening and the toning of the upper body muscles make pole walking especially attractive to women.

- ✓ The small expenditure for material and supplies makes pole walking accessible to anybody.
- ✓ Pole walking can be performed in any weather with the use of appropriate clothing.
- ✓ Pole walking is normally found to be less tiring than classic-style walking and is a lot more fun to do.
- ✓ Pole walking poles allow specific stretching and strengthening exercises to be performed, which would not be possible or effective enough without the poles. Having an exercise partner makes it possible to perform even more advanced exercises.
- ✓ The stretching and strengthening exercises with the poles, more specifically jumping and stepping routines, make the training interesting and versatile for beginning and advanced students alike.
- ✓ Pole walking is a very controllable body activity.

The intensity can be increased or decreased through the following methods:

- Interval walking (fast/slow)
- Use of hilly terrain
- Step and jump exercises (walking, jogging, jumping, etc.)
- The intensity of pressure used on the poles
- Strengthening exercises

This makes pole walking interesting enough for beginners as well as professional athletes as an addition to their routine fitness program or a good foundation for their base program.

Pole walking is ideal for beginners and people who are starting back again, and those who are looking for an activity that is less demanding than jogging but more intense and fun than walking.

Pole walking is now the fastest growing way to exercise across Europe for the masses. Germany has had an explosion in this area over the last 5 years, and the German designed Chung Shi walking shoe, using a completely different approach with a rocker sole, has increased the benefits that give you a program you can accomplish in minutes a day instead of hours. With increased benefits, including burning more calories and increased muscle toning and shaping, especially in the leg and buttock areas.

Obviously daily exercise is an important component for good health. The Pink Pole Balance Walking concept provides you with an option that will reduce your exercise time while, at the same time, increase benefits. This is an exercise program that is inexpensive and can be done all year long, with a group, alone or with your family.

It is a fun way to add fitness to you and your family's daily lives.

Do you like to walk with other people?

It's interactive, it's bonding, it's fun and fitness blended. Visit www.balancewalking.com to find a group near you!

Start a Balance Walking Club at work or in your neighborhood.

Getting Started

Before we get started on the Balance Walking technique, let's discuss the basic equipment you will need for your walk. It all starts with the poles. You cannot just use any poles; you will need a set that is specifically designed for Pink Pole Balance Walking.

Our recommendation to start this program would be to use the Pink Pole Adjustable Balance Walking Poles designed specifically for this program. For every pair of Pink Pole Balance Walking poles purchased, $5 will be donated to Susan G. Komen for the Cure®.

As the name suggests, they are adjustable and best of all they are very affordable. They will work well to get you started into the program without breaking the bank. In addition, Foot Solutions stores and our extensive network of coaches and mentors have a free introductory starter class with certified Balance Walking instructors. Visit www.balancewalking.com for coaches and/or www.footsolutions.com for more information on their walking program and the locations of their scheduled walks and stores. If you want to try this out before investing in any equipment Foot Solutions and Balance Walking coaches across the country provide loaner poles for your free lesson and walk. Try it. You'll like (perhaps love) it.

You can also purchase all your Balance Walking needs at a Foot Solutions store or online, if there is not a convenient location in your area.

Working with a certified trainer will remarkably improve your walking technique and performance.

However, if you are not located near a Foot Solutions store or one of the hundreds of trained coaches, we have a DVD available, as well as an online video, showcasing the basic techniques of Pink Pole Balance Walking. Once you purchase your poles you are ready to rock and roll!

Note: At the beginning to get started any good walking shoe will work. Although there are a lot of terrific shoes on the market, please understand I originally created the Balance Walking program in sync with our Chung Shi shoes. Can you proceed with your own choice of shoes? Yes! Do we recommend Chung Shi? Yes! Please visit www.footsolutions.com for more information.

Ready Position / Adjust Pole Parts

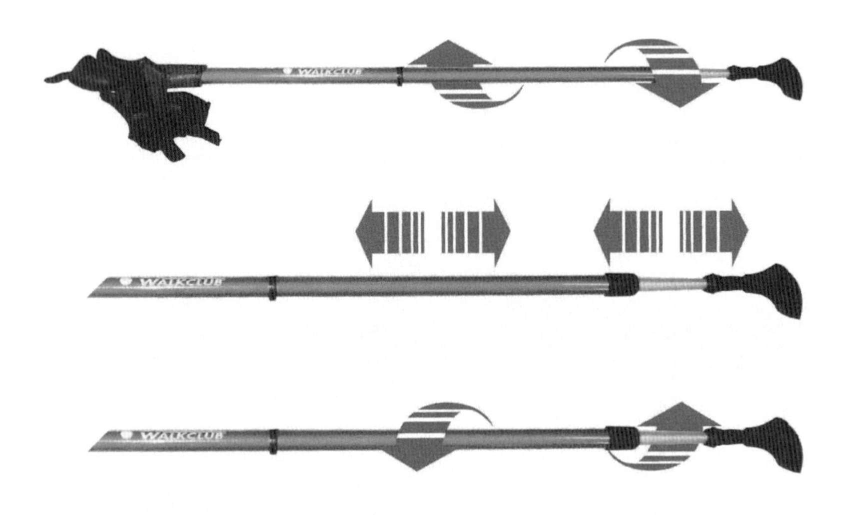

Simple adjustment to lengthen or shorten pole

Best Starting Pole Position (expert might adjust 90 degree at elbow plus an inch higher or intermediate/beginner 90 degrees minus 1-2 inches).

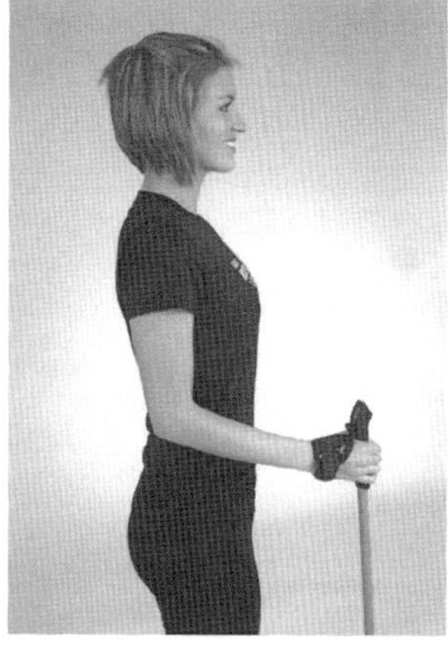

Start Here
HEALTH LEVEL
1" to 2" lower than 90 degrees

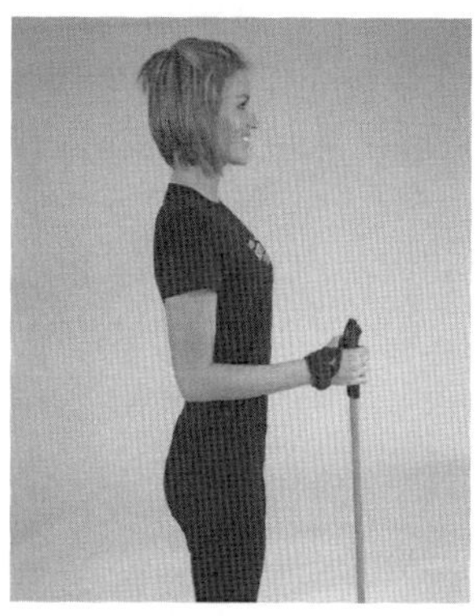

FITNESS LEVEL
90 degrees at elbow

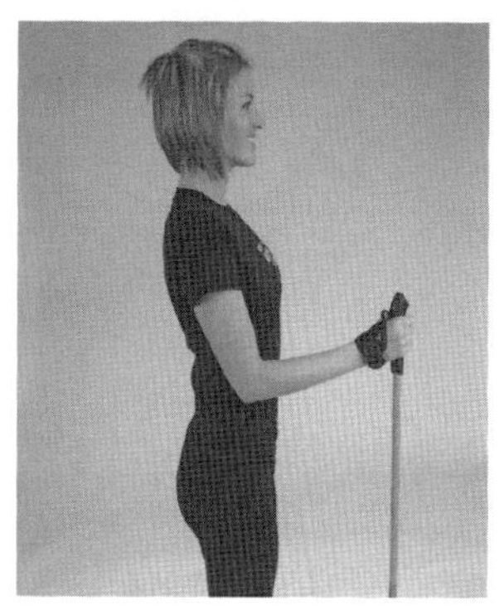

SPORT LEVEL
Adjustment for the experienced pole walker
1" to 2" higher than 90 degrees

Balance Walking – The Basics

(Simple Step By Step Instructions in a couple of minutes)

✓ Adjust your poles to the correct height:

a. The rule of thumb is if your pole is upright, your elbows will be at a 90 degree angle when grasping the hand grips.

b. At 90 degrees adjust pole heights based on your need level:

Health - 1-2 in. lower

Fitness - 90 deg. elbow

Sport - 1-2 in. higher

✓ Align rubber pole tips and adjust hand straps:

a. Align rubber pole tips to face angled back, or remove and use spike for grass or dirt.

b. Adjust hand straps so hands are comfortably snug against grip and have minimal play.

c. This strap adjustment is important in helping you minimize your over squeezing the grip on the poles. You will be cupping them in your hands as you begin walking with the poles. If you choose the advanced techniques you will be varying the gripping in coordination with the pole swing.

- ✓ Adjust Rubber Paws to face angled back, or remove & use spike for grass and dirt.

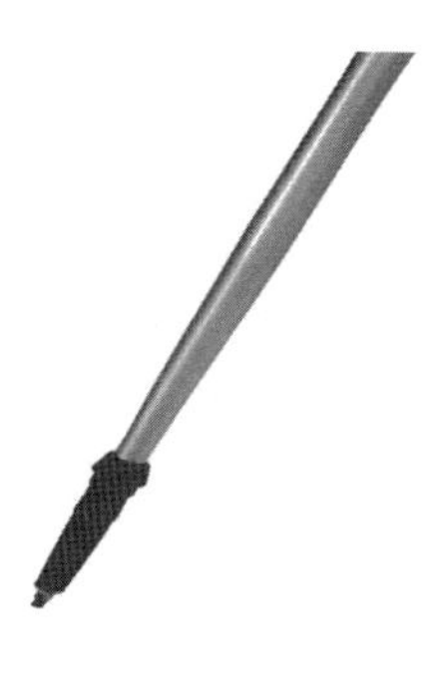

Rubber tip facing to rear

Remove tip for off road use

- ✓ Adjust Straps (hands comfortably snug against grip, so the grip and the release have minimal play). The closer your hand is to the pole when you have opened and released your hand in the push off phase the better.

Hand Grip Position

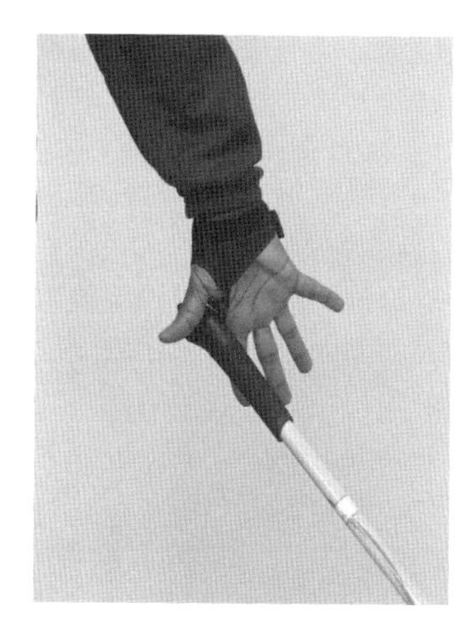

Hand release motion

To start, you will need to adjust the length of the poles for your body height. While holding the pole by the handle, stand it upright on the floor in front of you. With your upper arm near your side and elbow bent to a 90° angle, tighten the pole adjuster so that the handle is even with your hand and the pole is parallel with your body.

If you are a beginner, we recommend you lower the pole another one to two inches so that the pole length is just under the ninety-degree 90° mark. This is a great way to help get your arms accustomed to the poles. As you get the rhythm and hang of it you can adjust the poles to the 90° mark. Please note: If you are doing off-road walking you should lengthen poles slightly, based on the terrain and ground type, and remove the rubber tip booty. When putting the booty back on, it should always point to the rear. Note: The rubber tip booties are replaceable so don't get excited if you wear them down. In fact "wearing them down" means you're working (and walking) hard... or you're not Balance Walking correctly.

Once the poles have been adjusted, insert your thumbs into the hole of each wrist strap, paying attention to which is right and left, velcro them firmly, but comfortably around the wrist. The main purpose of the wrist strap is to allow the hand release techniques to be used properly while walking.

Warming up and Stretching

Balance Walking should always start with a warm-up to prepare your body for the walk and to help prevent injuries. The warm-up increases blood and oxygen circulation. In turn, this increases the flexibility of muscles and prepares you mentally and physically for your exercise session. Always breathe, move and stretch lightly before you walk for a nice warm up.

The walking poles are an excellent aid to increase your flexibility, strength and balance. Warm-up should start with a few minutes of walking and some warm-up exercises with your arms and shoulders; so with Balance Walking you can actually start right in walking without any additional warm-up. Just start off slow and pick up the pace when you are ready. It is recommended that stretching should not be done at the beginning of your exercise program, but saved for the end when muscles have been warmed up and have better elasticity. This is the time to stretch and work on flexibility.

For some of you that have been warming up and stretching before your workout let me suggest that this is obviously your option and choice. There are a number of stretches in the cool down section that can be used for warm ups also.

Since Pink Pole Balance Walking is a low impact exercise, I always use a slower warm up pace as my warm up. Again, time is the one area that most people do not have an excess of, so the warm up with the poles gives you the most effective use of time.

Poles and Basic Techniques

First of all, keep your body upright, make sure not to lean forward and relax your shoulders and arms. Then, loosen your grip on the poles and hang your hands down to your sides. Casually start walking without gripping your poles. At this point, you are dragging your poles behind you. Walk about ten to twenty yards so you can just get the feel of walking while dragging the poles.

Next, grasp your poles loosely in order to gain control of them then gently swing your arms while you walk.

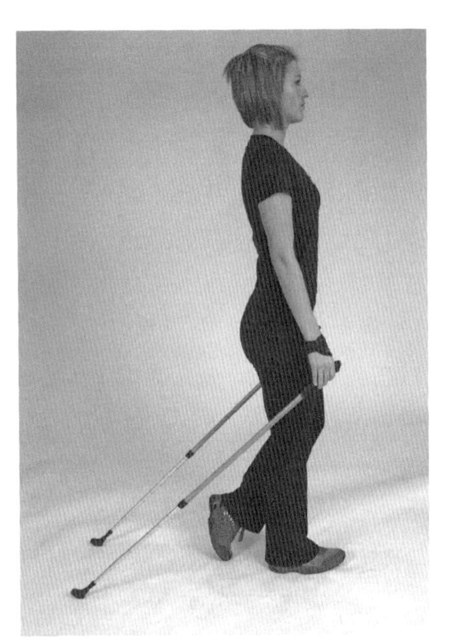

Always start by dragging the poles with hands straight down (not swinging)

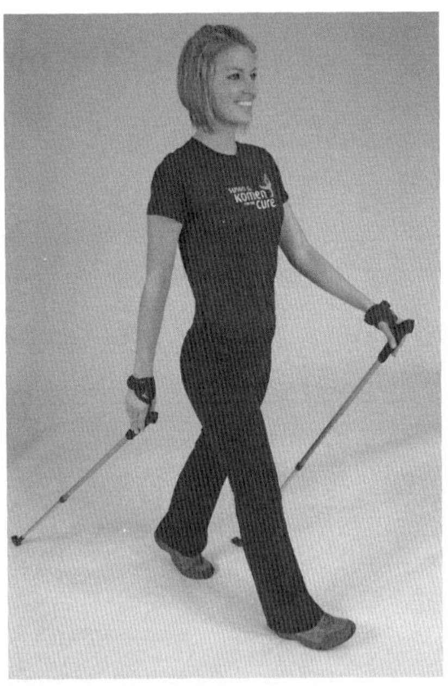

Swinging arms naturally (not gripping – yet as you progress and feel comfortable begin squeezing and releasing the grip)

Apply pressure to hand grips and against pole straps as you plant and stride.

NOTE: The pole tips should not extend past the front of your feet as you walk. You are not reaching out; you are just swinging your arms. Do this for several minutes until you feel comfortable with the motion. If at anytime you feel out of rhythm, go back to dragging the poles for several steps. Remember that your shoulders must be down and relaxed so you are still walking in the correct posture and not leaning forward.

A simple way for new people to start

Put your hands into the gloves and drop the poles behind you. Just walk and drag the poles behind you for 20 seconds. Once you get the rhythm, start to use your arms naturally, swing your arms with out holding the grips for another 20 seconds or more. Relax, smile and breathe. The poles will be a natural extension of your arms and hands. At the beginning a light grip on the hand grips is all that is needed.

Common beginner mistakes can include the following:

- Death grips on the poles creating tension up your arms & neck.
- Looking down at your feet, instead chin up, shoulders back & down
- Pulling the poles in front of your feet & body - you should always push behind you with the poles. Your arms are like the pistons in an engine. Push back, push back, and push back. Swing your arms like pendulums from the shoulder, do not pump with the elbows and carry the poles in front of you.
- Most novice pole walkers might wrongly use the same leg with the same pole. It feels weird and almost off balance. It should be opposite hand to meet the opposite foot. Just don't THINK ABOUT IT! Your body will know how to adapt and do it. When you get off the beat, just stop and drag again for a while. It is not unusual to spend a long time in the beginner phase here. You have to start some place even experienced pole walkers have to stop and drag to get the motion back. Once you've got it, its intuitive, fun and a fabulous workout.

1 – 2 – 3 Sequential Technique

1. Swing – Reach – Squeeze
2. Plant – Press – Propel
3. Stride – Push - Release

Fine Tuning / Correcting Your Technique

- Pole presses back 45 degrees while leaning slightly forward (this creates a straight line with arm and pole shaft).
- Pole tip at forward most point of swing is between feet (not in front of feet).
- Close and open grip with each step which is attained with more experience.
- Elbows should swing close to body (like train tracks)

Uphill Technique

- Lean forward slightly
- Reach out longer with poles
- Push back strong to power up the hill

Downhill Technique

- Softer knees
- Feet flatter on the ground
- Lean slightly back (apply more downward pressure to pole straps)

Advanced Technique

- Hands close at plant and open at push
- Double poles
- Zig Zag or Skating
- Jogging
- Running
- Jumping strides

Increase Core Temperature

With and/or without poles, you can increase the range of motion by grasping the poles above the head as well as using the poles to support standing wall stretch. The basics are provided in support materials.

As you move the pole forward, plant and push off. At this point, the pole should be just above the ground and planted approximately one foot behind your lead foot. Your arms should not be fully extended, but slightly bent at the elbows. Walk like this until you feel very comfortable with your rhythm and stride.

The next step takes a little practice to get used to, but is a very important step to master. Remember, the pole is held with a comfortable grip. This is important. Your grip should start to tighten just before you move the pole forward and plant it through the push-off. You then release grip as the pole moves behind you. This takes a little getting used to for most people. The more you think about it, the more you struggle with this phase. Just keep walking and let the grip-and-release technique come naturally. Be patient, it will come.

Mastering the grip-and-release technique is an important part of the process in order for you to achieve the full effect from your Pink Pole Balance Walking workout. Again, don't worry about it - the grip-and-release will come to you in time. The best thing is to not think about it, let it happen naturally.

Once you are comfortable with your rhythm, you can concentrate more on swinging your arms and actually get your shoulders into the arm-swinging movement. Again, your body and shoulders should be in a relaxed, correct posture position.

Congratulations! You have just mastered the basic Pink Pole Balance Walking technique!

Remember, Balance Walking is a low-impact fitness walking system used to create a total body workout without taking a toll on your body or mind and without requiring hours of workout. You will be working the large muscle groups of both your upper and lower body. Along with toning your arms, shoulders, chest, buttocks and leg muscles, you will also be getting a heart pumping cardiovascular workout. This is a program that provides you many benefits without pushing yourself. Balance Walking will improve your whole body as well as the state of your mind.

The basic Pink Pole Balance Walking technique is simple and can be learned in a couple of minutes.

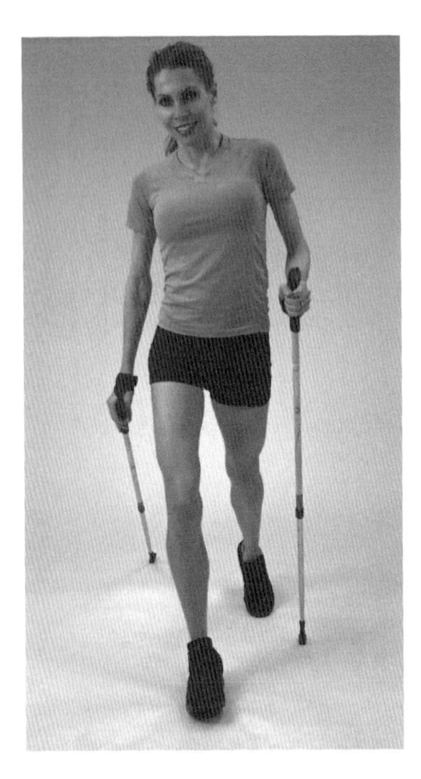

1. Adjust your poles to the correct height.

2. Align the pole tips and adjust the hand straps.

3. Pole Walking Position.

4. Begin walking normally as you drag the poles.

5. Once you feel tension in the hand grips, grip then release the poles.

Balance Walking can be done anywhere, anytime and during any season, which is what is so great about this form of exercise.

If weather is a problem, the mall is a great place to walk. Most malls have walking times from 7am to 10am, before the stores open. Also, many fitness clubs, YMCA's and even large corporate offices have walking, jogging or running tracks indoors.

We have walked in covered parking lots, airports etc. Use your imagination, be creative, you'll find a place.

You will notice the rubber tips located on the end of your walking poles. These are removable for off-road walking in rough terrain, on a trail or in the snow. The rubber tips are also easily replaced, should they become worn or damaged.

Again, here are some common beginner's mistakes to watch out for:

- ✓ 'Death grips' on the poles will create tension up your arms and neck. Looking down at your feet will affect your posture. Have your chin up, shoulders back and relaxed.
- ✓ Putting the poles in front of your feet and body – You should always push behind you with the poles, instead of reaching and extending your arms like pistons in an engine – push, push, push.
- ✓ Wrongly using the same leg with the same pole, making your stride feel weird and off. Just as with regular walking, each hand should meet its opposite foot to keep your stride in balance.
- ✓ Thinking too hard about the movement. Your body will know how to do it because it is natural.

Pink Pole Balance Walking is not difficult. You already have fifty percent of it down if you know how to walk! However, there are some things to which you must pay attention. You will want to maintain correct upright posture; be sure not to reach out with the poles and do not over-extend your step. This is more about finesse and proper technique.

Remember, when you get off the beat, just stop moving the poles and drag the poles again for several minutes until you get your rhythm back. There is no rush and no competition. Just keep going back to basics whenever needed. Even experienced Balance Walkers have to just drag their poles to get the rhythm back. Once you've got it, it's intuitive, fun and a fabulous workout.

Now, let's get into some additional techniques that you will find useful as you expand your program. We don't call this 'raising the bar.' We refer to it as 'raising the pole.'

Pink Pole Balance Walking – Fast Mode

Athletes find Balance Walking a great change up.

Speeding up your pace should not cause you to break form; you still want to maintain good posture and rhythm. You are not taking bigger steps; you are taking faster steps. This means that your body rhythm must keep up with your feet. This is natural and once you have mastered the basic Balance Walking technique, it should not be a problem. A great way to practice this is with short interval training.

Walk with a fast pace for a few minutes then fall back to a regular pace for eight minutes. As your stamina increases, you can adjust your speed interval (increased walking pace) accordingly. Remember, this is not a race. It is all about you, how you feel and what you want to accomplish with your Pink Pole Balance Walking routine. Mix it up, change the pace, change the place you walk occasionally, do it on vacation, when travelling; establish your habit now.

Balance Walking - Jogging

Yes, you can increase the tempo to a light jog, again using the poles for rhythm and control. You can occasionally throw in a light jog if you wish to increase your workout pace or level. This is not necessary or required. I only mention it for the aggressive exercisers who always want to push the envelope and themselves. The poles can be used effectively to take some of the strain off your knees and back - which is one of the reasons injured runners like it.

In addition we have used this program with wounded soldiers and with pre and post surgery patients. Pink Pole Balance Walking is great, therefore for pre-hab and re-hab.

Reach out programs to the military.

Balance Walking – Gliding

This occurs when you are gracefully gliding (think of a gazelle-like action) one foot to the other. In this case, you are almost running, but moving more smoothly with less of an impact on your joints. Again, this will get your heart rate up and is suggested only for the physically fit who want to take it to the highest level.

For the competition junkie, fast mode, jogging and gliding will test your endurance and the rest of your body. For most of us, good-old, basic Balance Walking with some speed intervals will be enough.

When walking with other people, it is important for the group to break up into Balance Walking levels. It's best to have slower beginners in one group and advanced in another. This allows people to enjoy the walk at a level appropriate for their skill set and their individual goals. Walking groups and partners make the walks more entertaining; I have actually held business meetings and discussions during walks that have been very fruitful. Since I am an acknowledged workaholic, I feel like I am taking care of two issues at the same time. Talk about efficiency! Some call it 'multi-tasking', I call it efficiency! Think about a light lunch and Balance Walk for 15 minutes or more, it's a much better meeting than the typical passive chow down meeting.

Balance Walking – Up Hill

While going uphill, place the body in a position that is bent slightly forward and plant the pole alongside your lead foot. You will be using your arms and upper-body strength more while putting the added pressure on the poles. Your whole body will get a more aggressive workout. As a result, hills should be included in your workouts as you progress.

Balance Walking – Down Hill

What goes up must come down. Going downhill requires shorter steps. Also, the poles should be planted just in front of the foot and with the added pressure you're putting on the pole, less pressure will be placed on the legs and knees which is especially beneficial to those with bad or weak knees.

The basic Balance Walking techniques will allow you to safely walk at your own pace and on any terrain, whereas the more advanced techniques are designed to bring your workout to the next level. Remember, the primary principle of the poles is not only to increase your workout intensity by using 90% of your muscles, but will allow you to use the poles to take the pressure and weight off the rest of your body and help with core stability.

This balancing effect allows you to participate in a program even if you are overweight, have minor mobility problems or medical issues. You can be young or old, in great shape or just trying to find your way back to a healthy lifestyle.

Remember, this program is about you and your present activity level. Put balance back into your life with a Balance Walking program that is designed for your needs and level of activity.

Warm Up - Cool Down

This is an important part of your program and can be as simple as winding down your walk for the last several minutes and finishing with some basic stretching techniques. Stretching is best performed when your body is thoroughly warmed up. Gentle stretching will help you stay flexible and more youthful.

However, if desired you can use the same techniques for a warm up before you get started. My preference is to build my warm up right into my walk then stretch during cool down.

Balance Walking and Cool Down

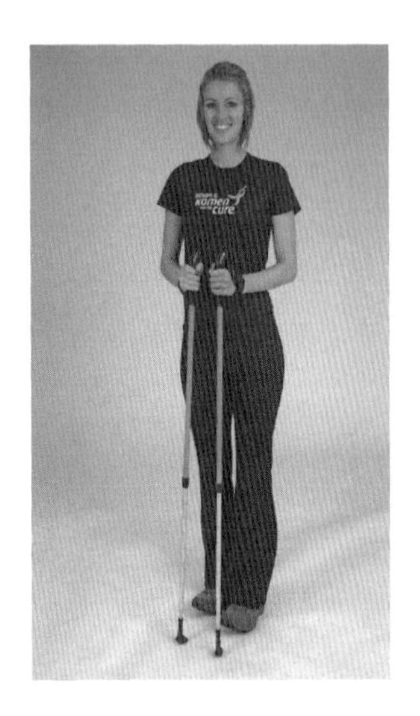

It's best to begin by learning good technique with a qualified instructor or highly experienced fitness advocate, who can easily pinpoint your difficulties while helping you correct them quickly, before you risk an injury. Because of the repetition in your routine, we want to break bad habits before they injure you. Your Balance Walking coach can help you. At least, review this approach and visit the Balance Walking website.

Stretching and Flexibility

As we age the joints don't move and function as well as they did when we were younger. This is why the Cool-Down exercises are almost as important as the Balance Walking itself. Because these exercise movements below are completed using poles they become your surest way to measure your bodies starting level, and, of course, the body's changes after a great session. This is all about stretching and flexibility. Definitely an area most people ignore as they age. Also, I am a strong advocate of stretching at the end of your session. There are a lot of studies that support that premise but if you think about it your muscles are warmed up and there is much less chance of injury when stretching at this time.

Note: For ease of movement as you stretch with the poles, it is not necessary to have your hands strapped in. Simply stretch holding the grip.

First, the warm-up will increase circulation, heat the muscles and joints, and result in much more fluid movement. My recommendation is your warm-up should be your actual Balance Walk just at a slower pace. Remember time is time and I want you Balance Walking for 15 minutes every day.

Second, the cool-down is important to prevent lactic acid buildup, resulting in stiffness that would interfere with how you feel. Remember any changes in how you start, where and when you walk, how long, how vigorous all impact differences in one session over another. If it works for you, continue the practice. If not, find another method.

Here are some cool down stretches to incorporate into your routine. Just do a few after each Balance Walking session and mix them up to stretch out your whole body. For more stretches and exercises visit our website.

Remember, a Body in Motion tends to stay in Motion. Therefore get off the couch and get moving.

Flexibility - key to a youthful look and feel.

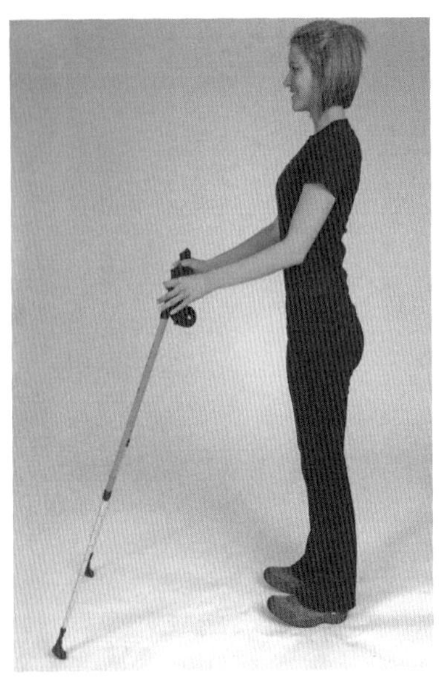

Glute Stand and Lunge

- Poles planted just beyond arms length, shoulder width.
- Take generous step forward, firmly planting foot and kneeling on back leg.
- The lead leg is the gauge of up to a 90 degree knee bend, at a comfortable range.
- Push away from your lead foot while using your poles to come back to starting position. Repeat each leg 5 times. The use of poles helps you also use arms, shoulder & chest muscles.

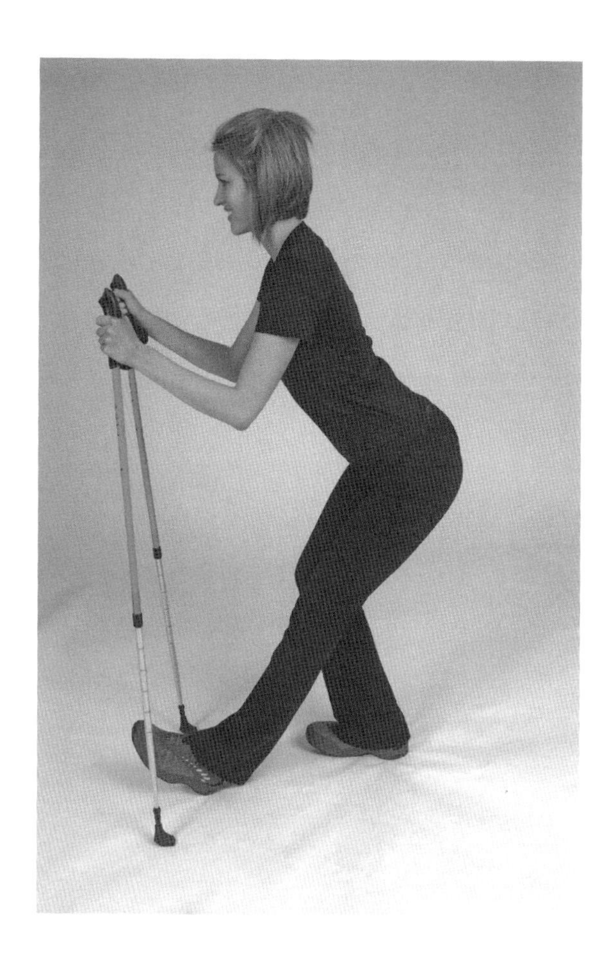

Calf and Hamstring Stretch

- Poles planted at arms length, shoulder width.
- Place one heel just behind pole plant, keep leg straight in front with toes pointing up. You can use the pole - pressing against the pole for a greater stretch.
- Bend your other knee while leaning forward with a straight back. Be careful and gentle.
- Hold for about 10 seconds on each leg.

Back Stretch

- Plant poles just past arms length at a shoulder width.
- Keep arms straight lean on poles.
- Bend at the waist keeping your back straight. Avoid hyper-extending.
- Breath easy in and out through motion. Hold for about 10 to 15 seconds. This definitely feels good – especially for the lower back.

Balance Walking is truly a low-impact activity that is enjoyed by all fitness levels.

From the couch potato to the elite athlete in training, Balance Walking will help get you into the best condition of your life. It is very effective for pre-op training and post-op recovery.

Sometimes we have to help ourselves to give us the best opportunity life has to offer.

CHAPTER 2

STRESS REDUCTION

Stress

Everyone experiences some level of stress daily, weekly, throughout our lives. Let's face it, there are often changes in our lives that cause various levels of stress. The loss of a loved one, the fear of the unknown, a medical issue or trauma, relocation, divorce, work, overload, children, challenges, or, just life itself... it's all part of the game of life.

How you deal with stress as an individual will determine its impact on you and your loved ones. Some people create a lot of stress on themselves by constantly ignoring worst case scenarios. Also, stress is self-induced.

Negativity in life seems to attract negative results. Try not to get yourself all worked up until you have all the facts. No matter what the situation is, always try to visualize the positive side of it. Positive energy is good and will help you get through most crises.

Create balance in your life by paying attention to your needs in a positive way. These should include all of your needs - physical, intellectual, emotional, family, spiritual and social. This will be a great place to start.

There is no shortage of stress. As many as 3 out of 4 people in the US today state they are frazzled, anxious, nervous, and stressed. Stress has been called 'the silent killer.' It takes an unbelievable toll on the human body. By the way, if weight is a problem for you and you cannot reduce your stress level you will never change the weight problem. That's a fact!

Beating or controlling stress is necessary if you are going to survive in today's world. Stress is a major factor in obesity, as well as many diseases including cancer, heart disease, high blood pressure, Type 2 diabetes, headache, insomnia, depression, anxiety, dementia and the aging process. Reducing or eliminating stress is a very important part of the Pink Pole Balance Walking Program. There are many ways to do this, so let's go over some approaches that could work for you.

In many cases, stress is self influenced, possibly by simply living in or longing for the past or being concerned about the future; which can turn into a mind game trying to figure everything out and anticipate everything that may or may not happen. In many cases, it is only our thoughts that distract us from what's really important or from enjoying the moment.

Some simple ways to attack STRESS head on:

✓ One of the most effective ways is exercise, especially a program that allows your mind to relax and not focus on the negative thoughts. Regularly drinking green or black tea or eating a small piece of dark chocolate.

✓ Create some quiet time for yourself; as little as 5 minutes a day of quiet time, where you think of nothing at all; this is form of meditation. You can actually meditate if you so choose.

- ✓ Laughter is also a great way to reduce and eliminate stress. There are many studies that support these statements on laughter. In short, happiness (through laughter) relaxes your body. Believe it or not, laughing is good for you! A great reason to enjoy a good laugh is that it instantaneously produces health benefits; watching funny movies, comedians, anything that allows you to actually really laugh. Let it loose, don't think about it enjoy the freedom and the moment.

- ✓ Try Yoga, Tai Chi, listening to calming music, doing anything that takes the edge off and gives your mind a break from reality. Meditation could be traditional or it could be as simple as repeating a prayer over and over to yourself. What it does is put your mind in a simple state of relaxation.
- ✓ Stop focusing on the negative and think about the positive. Negative people have a way of pulling everyone down and the worst thing is you cannot change them. Are you getting enough sleep? Do you have a strong social support network you can confide in? Sometimes just talking about it helps.
- ✓ Sometimes all it takes is a pet that helps you achieve that quiet time especially if you live alone.

A pet becomes a buddy and will take your mind off many things. If you don't have a pet, maybe you should.

- ✓ Watching the tranquility of a fish tank is another great escape.

- ✓ Today you can get DVDs that will give you every relaxing setting you can think of from ocean reefs to mountain tops back to a relaxing brook.
- ✓ Everyone gets pulled in too many different directions – family, work, house, community to name a few. Most people are overwhelmed. We are way too busy chasing the dream that very few of us are enjoying the trip. By the way, the journey is what everything is about.
- ✓ If you are a procrastinator, stay focused and start selecting each task that needs to be completed and accomplish them one at a time. Set aside some time each day to get a project completed.
- ✓ At work if you are overwhelmed, delegate.

You can't do everything yourself even if you believe that you are the only one who can do it. On those tasks you need to get done, focus on the most important one first. Most people put off the most important task that needs to get done - filling their time with the simple easy work. By prioritizing and staying focused, this will reduce the source of stress substantially. Most people focus on the little easy things to get done and procrastinate on the more important difficult problems.

Remember, eat the big frog first.

DON'T BE A STRESS EATER; you will pack on pounds and for some reason stress poundage accumulates at your belly. This is the unhealthiest place to pack it on. This is the one area I have the most problem with. A bad day at work, heavy travel schedule, it is so easy to wolf down a second helping or focus on comfort foods that I have been trying to avoid like the plague.

There are many articles and studies now available on the direct relationship between stress and excessive weight gain, as well as loss. In addition, there are a number of studies relating stress to many illnesses. Although this makes sense, many of us are unaware of how to relieve this burden by minimizing stress to prevent such health problems.

The answer? Think positively instead of negatively. How long do you think it took me to come up with that one? How simple could it be? Think about it; just look around you at the people you know. We all know at least one person that, for some reason, deals with one life crisis after another. But when you look closer, they are constantly either thinking or talking negatively. It seems their worst fears just continue to happen. Then, there are the chosen ones. Everything they seem to do just works out, they are always positive and take the downside in stride, but seem to turn even negative events into positive ones. There is actually a bigger theory here, and again, it is very simple. Be careful what you ask for because you might get it. But you can't just ask for it; you must believe it. I'm talking about a way of life. It may not show up tomorrow, but if you are positive enough, it will happen. If you get a chance, listen to "The Secret" by Rhonda Byrne. This re-enforces everything I believe in and pretty much is how I have lived my whole life.

This all started with stress and how stress impacts a person's life. Pink Pole Balance Walking also includes some suggestions on how to make stress reduction a regular part of your life and certainly is a critical part of the complete program.

Achieving wellness in one's life is not difficult. Let's begin with common sense and take ownership of our lives. Our stressful lifestyles contribute significantly to the 'fix' predicament we are in today. Part of your every day must be dedicated to stress reduction. Fortunately, Pink Pole Balance Walking itself, especially if you incorporate meditative walking, could have a big impact on your stress levels.

Just 5 minutes a day of quiet time can have a very effective calming impact on your stress levels. Try to set a schedule and do it the same time every day and at the same place.

Here is a simple way to get started:

1. Find a peaceful place to sit and relax. Play soft meditative music or sounds of nature, the ocean, brook or even rain, whatever is what is relaxing to you.

2. Breathe slowly in and out. Try belly breathing like a baby – let your stomach rise and fall with each breath. First, inhale deeply through your nose filling your lungs from the bottom up. Start with your belly, then mid lungs, then finally upper lungs. Hold for several seconds, then release. Exhale reversing the process. This may feel odd at first but you will easily get the rhythm.

3. Close your eyes and try not to think about anything but the moment. For me, thinking about floating in water is most effective, while some people like to float in air. What is important here is you are not thinking about anything. Sometimes a mantra will help or even a repetitive prayer. It simply puts your mind, in a suspense-like state.

4. When I finish a session, I like to rub my hands together to warm them up, then, place them over my eyes. It is a simple way to end the session while feeling very relaxing and energizing at the same time.

On stress busting, there are many ways you can approach this. Be optimistic and positive in the way you act and think; it works. Learn to accept life when a situation is out of your control, learn to let it go. Focus on the things you can change, not the things you can't.

Part of your Pink Pole Balance Walking routine can be a reflective walk by yourself once or twice a week in a peaceful setting for you. It could simply be sitting for 5 to 10 minutes while allowing your mind to settle into a tranquil state. Some people listen to soothing sounds of nature, some people may repeat a prayer or a mantra; it could be new age music or some of the old masters.

These approaches all have the same effect on the mind. If you want to really open your mind, you may consider going traditional with one of the many forms of meditation.

Tai Chi is considered a moving meditation with low impact, non-combative movements to build strength and create structural balance in the body.

The list is endless; the point is to take a few minutes everyday. Let's say 5 minutes of quiet time.

You can test the calming effects of meditation very simply. Start in a comfortable position, in a quiet or serene place that is dimly lit or shaded. At this time you may not want to lie down because sleeping is not meditation.

The process starts with relaxed breathing as described earlier, as you start to relax, gently close your eyes and continue the breathing and relaxing for 5 to 10 minutes. You may use a mantra or sound to keep you focused in the moment. When thoughts wander in, let them move through, do not dwell on them. Sometimes picturing yourself floating through the air or water will help you move into a deeper state of relaxation or maybe laying down in a field of grass and wild flowers.

Please note: some people react differently to this approach. You should go with the approach that feels the most comfortable to you and relaxes you. I prefer the floating through water but that is probably because of my love of the ocean and water. If you use a mantra continue to repeat it slowly in your mind.

As you end your meditation or quiet time, wind down slowly, rub your hands together and place the palms over your eyes before opening them. Feel the warmth of your palms, soothing and relaxing, then, wipe your face with your hands while feeling the warmth and glow of your own body.

It sounds crazy, but it works as a healing process that will substantially reduce stress and give you new energy and life.

With Yoga and Tai Chi, there is no strain; you work to the level that is right for your body. People well into their 80's are performing Tai Chi daily, as it forms a beautiful, slow dance based on the martial arts. These forms of mind and body control and relaxation have been around for centuries. Look to the wisdom of the Far East. If they did not work, people would not still be doing them.

Benefits are:

1. Healthy Body

- Develop physical power
- Improve strength and flexibility
- Manage weight
- Relieve pain
- Sleep better
- Stimulate the immune system
- Lower blood pressure and cholesterol levels
- Slow the heart rate
- Reverse the effects of aging

2. Happy Mind

- Find emotional serenity
- Release stress
- Become centered and balanced
- Reverse depression and anxiety
- Improve focus and concentration

3. Peaceful Spirit

- Awaken spiritual energy
- Increase self-awareness and self-acceptance
- Foster inner joy and happiness
- Enhance personal relationships
- Discover inner peace

Remember, it is important to treat everyone with respect and consideration; you should be at the top of your list. There is absolutely no reason why you should not love yourself.

Why do I suggest some form of stress relief through meditation or just simple mind relaxation? This is part of the lifestyle change that will have a positive impact on you and everyone you come in contact with.

Flexibility is one of the keys to reversing the process of aging and among some of the major components to living the Pink Pole Balance Walking Way. Remember we are talking about lifestyle changes you can live with that can help you have a fuller, more active, healthier life.

Maybe for you it is a massage and a day at the spa.

Start your meditation/brain relaxing program for 5 minutes a day. If you like the change and benefits increase to 10 minutes a day.

Are you ready to renew, re-energize and recreate? Treat yourself once a week with a relaxing body massage. Discover the natural healing power of Dahn Yoga, a dynamic exercise program rooted in the ancient wisdom of Korea. You will learn to accumulate and circulate energy through your body while calming and clarifying your mind, creating a happier, more healthy and peaceful life.

The following "Introduction to Yoga" has been made available to me from author Kimberly Hard.

Kimberly is also the Founder & CEO of Be Well Atlanta which is a great networking group for all organizations affiliated with health and wellness programming.

Kimberly has spent years teaching yoga in the wellness community with cancer patients and survivors. The meditation part of yoga has been very beneficial and helpful to many of the patients she has worked with.

Kimberly has also brought yoga to the Atlanta Aquarium which has literally opened up a whole new experience for both the Beluga whales and the yoga class.

Relaxing the Body

In the beginning, relax the body. Inhale and with the exhalation, release tension. Inhale, and with the following exhalation scan the body from top to bottom and from the bottom upwards.

Wherever there is gripping or tension – relax.

The mind is looking at the body with a parental eye. With time, one can observe tense areas releasing and embracing space. If areas of weakness are noticed, inhale into them with courage and enliven them with energy. Let excess leave the body; relax. Thus the body becomes stable and quiet.

Yoga can provide strength and toning as well as stress relief.

Quieting the Mind

When we position ourselves on the mat, we distance ourselves from our responsibility to react to the world. The eyes look inward to catch the inner mood, the state of mind.

Whether we are concentrated, dispersed or nervous; happy, sad or angry; whether we are afraid, tired or energetic – the eyes are positioned at the back of the head.

We observe ourselves and our practice from an inner silence. With each inhalation the eyes sink deeper into the back of the head. With each exhalation there is an intensification of concentration.

Empty mind intensifies itself in practice.

Intent

Now the body and mind are at ease and stable, quiet and concentrated. From this place we see our objective – Sitting, Pranayama, Asana – and direct ourselves toward it.

The mind directs itself to the practice; the body awaits the practice; the heart embraces the practice with all its might.

With each inhalation there is an intensification of intent, with each exhalation the sharpening of its direction. By visualizing ourselves sitting, breathing, moving, or by imagining another person in that practice we devote ourselves wholly to it. With each breath, with each pose we reaffirm our intent.

People who are stressed on a regular basis are much more likely to suffer from illness than those who focus on the now and do not stress about things in their past or future. The solution is to stay focused on things you can change and control, instead of the things you can't. During stressful times, especially when you can actually feel the stress, take 5 minutes focusing on your breathing technique in order to quickly relax and calm yourself.

During the course of everyone's life there will be some tough times. It could be illness, a loss of a loved one, divorce, loss of a job, financial setbacks etc. We all have said "can it get any worse?"

Actually, it can – no matter how bad it is there is always something worse that can happen and no matter how good it is it could always be better.

Think of a storm with heavy winds. It is not the strong oak that normally survives but a tree that bends and sways with the wind.

Resiliency is critical in how we survive and adjust to those times when you will be tested.

Pink Pole Balance Walking will help provide you with buffers against stress and is a great step in moving forward. Finding positive meaning in things you do will also be very helpful.

Reaching out to friends, family and support groups are very helpful. You can be a support person, and helping someone else is like charging your own batteries.

Being more active spiritually can also help no matter what you believe. This is a time to look deep inside of yourself. Spiritual comfort comes in many ways. Finding the path that is best for you is what is important. Sometimes you can live more in one week than you can in a year. Most of us wander this earth without thinking about time, even though it is the most precious gift we have. Use it wisely when you finally realize how precious it really is.

Always find the positive in every problem or issue. See the opportunities that exist, they are all around us all the time. You have made a difference – don't stop now, someone can always make a difference.

LIVE EACH DAY!

Do something special for yourself or a loved one, or anyone. It could be something very small. Just do it! TODAY!

CHAPTER 3

FOOD FOR LIFE

Choosing foods by colors - reds, yellows, greens and purples will keep you focused on healthy, nutritious vegetables and fruits.

Don't stop here! My philosophy is to eat whatever you desire, just eat slower and enjoy each bite. Whatever it is, just eat half a portion.

Balance Walking and Food

As we all know, there is a great deal of data available on diets and quick weight loss programs. However, over time, they just do not work. My heritage is Italian and as I was growing up, food was an important part of the family and was so different than what meal time is like today.

It was an opportunity for family and friends to spend time together and talk. The food was great tasting and fresh. There was plenty of food to eat but no-one gorged themselves. It was about enjoying the moment; nothing like today where everything is a rush and we eat more processed food than anything else.

So, let's start by eliminating the word "diet" and stop thinking about it. How about using common sense instead?

Part of the problem is when you start playing games with food and try all the shortcut methods to lose weight; you actually throw off the natural balance of your body. The real secret to success in this area is not really a secret at all. It is simple: eat and enjoy life! Over time, your eating habits should evolve to adjust to your particular body needs. Food is one of the great pleasures of life and punishing yourself is just not going to work.

What does work? It is quite simple. Consider a form of grazing. For example, try eating smaller meals four to five times per day. Another option would be to have three meals a day with small snacks in between and before bedtime, to keep the fire burning.

If weight is an issue for you, eat six times a day. You can double your fat loss with this technique. My philosophy is to eat anything you want, just really savor every bit and have smaller portions.

Breakfast - the one meal you should NEVER miss!

Sometimes a fruit smoothie is the answer. Quick, healthy and tastes great!

It is well documented that eating breakfast will help you lose weight and actually keep you from gorging yourself later. Also, if you feel as though you need to eat a large meal everyday, be sure to make it lunch instead of at the end of the day, similar to what they do in the Mediterranean countries. Or better yet, if you think of the way the farmer eats - up early, huge breakfast, worked a long hard day but also eat smaller meals the rest of the day. Let us take a look at the single biggest issue in eating - portion control and the amount of chemicals and fillers in the food we eat today.

On a recent trip to Italy, I had wonderful meals that were so tasty and fresh but the key was they were reasonable portions and they used fresh ingredients. I did not hesitate to eat anything and never felt stuffed like I normally do here in the US. In addition, it has been well documented that drinking red wine is healthy. In fact, the longest living Europeans drink red wine their whole lives and yes, I drank wine at every meal and it felt great! I actually not only felt great and ate whatever I wanted on this trip, when I returned home I noticed I had also lost weight. How good is this? So why did I have to leave the country to enjoy eating less, and feeling better, and also lose weight?

Sticking with an exercise and eating plan that you can live with is what Pink Pole Balance Walking is all about. This is a lifelong decision and does not end when you reach your goal. Losing weight and getting in shape short-term is easy. It is keeping the weight off and staying in shape over time that becomes the challenge. When you have medical concerns, issues or problems it is even more important for you to take care of yourself and focus on your food.

My Greek friend, Gus - fresh figs, cheese & wine.
No, this is not Greece, it is his backyard on the outskirts of Atlanta!

NEVER DIET AGAIN

- ✓ Stop emotional eating
- ✓ Eat whatever you want
- ✓ Eat smaller portions
- ✓ Eat often
- ✓ Achieve your ideal weight
- ✓ Smaller plates
- ✓ More liquid
- ✓ Think taste & quality
- ✓ Don't make this an issue

Remember diets don't work – enjoy life and make changes and adjustments you can live with.

Forget about low fat and substitute chemicals. Think natural and eat real foods instead of trying to trick your body with substitutes that are not healthy for you and really don't accomplish anything. Just look around you at all the wonder diets, pills and low-fat products. If they are working, how come obesity is increasing instead of decreasing? Learn how to read labels and understand what you are putting into your body. Remember, chemical substitutes that replace the real thing are not acceptable. You are better off eating the real thing just be reasonable and savor the taste.

If you want to change your life and live a more, healthy, full lifestyle, then you have to be willing to make these simple commitments. Enjoy Pink Pole Balance Walking for as little as 15 minutes a day.

Do it every day, make it your routine and escape. Add to this a reasonable eating program that you can enjoy. Remember, eating breakfast and snacks along with small meals will actually give you remarkable results. Remember, we are talking about a lifestyle change. This is not a quick fix, but an investment in yourself for the way you will live the rest of your life.

In most cases, the issue is portion control.

There are many ways to overcome this problem.

Learn to recognize a reasonable portion size. The size of your palm is equal to one portion size. Most meals are comprised of 3 portions which include 1 protein, 1 vegetable and 1 natural grain. If you want to eat more, it needs to be vegetables.

Also, use smaller plates instead of oversized ones like those used in restaurants that serve huge meals. Unfortunately, in the United States, it is more about quantity than quality. Cut your portions in half and save the other half for another meal.

Also, take your time while eating. Try tasting and chewing, your food, instead of 'wolfing' it down. Give your body a chance to let you know it is no longer hungry. Drink water before and during your meal. Most Asian cultures have a cup of soup before their meals and drink hot tea with their meals. Traditional Chinese meals are not heavy but are loaded with vegetables. Also, simple things like setting up your plate with proper portions, remember to use smaller plates so the meal looks bigger and to eat slowly – really taste it and enjoy it.

Put your food away or set up several meals for future use and put them away so you won't take another helping. Family style eating will not work for you at this time. Family-style works if you use the Chinese approach; it's about the taste; you take a small serving from each plate. If you don't, there won't be anything left for the rest of the group. It is about experiencing the many wonderful tastes and textures. If you do have an opportunity to eat with a traditional Chinese family, they always take small portions and insure the elders at the table get first choice. It is a great tradition and will earn you respect. It does take restraint. My wife is Chinese, and the first time I ate with her family, it was struggle for me not to take bigger portions. It was a good thing I understood their customs, because I wanted to make a good impression. It would have been very easy to make a mistake. My background is Italian and we attack our food and add loaves of crusty Italian bread and dip it in olive oil and spices. Mama Mia that is so good!

If weight is a problem for you, weigh yourself every day. It is best to weigh yourself at the same time of each day for consistency, (i.e. every morning).

There will be small fluctuations - the key is to keep them small by adjusting your lifestyle accordingly.

However, be sure you do not obsess over ounces.

You are catching small changes as they occur so that your weight does not spiral out of control.

Stop punishing yourself if you eat something you enjoy. Instead, learn to celebrate the moment and to enjoy each occasional indulgence in moderation.

Fruit is a great indulgence. Eat it often.

If you don't, you will even eat more thinking it may be the last time you will eat this. It won't be! The more you make of it, the harder it will become to control and the urge will become a constant struggle. Trying to eliminate your favorite foods is the wrong approach. You will always feel deprived. You are much better off eating it but sensibly. Try eating sensible portions and really take your time chewing the food thoroughly, enjoying the taste and the texture. Slow yourself down; life is simple. Try to learn good eating habits, but know that it is okay to indulge occasionally, provided that you make the most of the moment.

When it comes to steering clear of certain items, make sure over-processed flour and sugar are at the top of your list, as well as heavily processed foods with fillers. Most of these products seem to settle at the waist. The eating issue is really very simple, you either burn and process what you eat, or it will stay with you until you do. The better level of fuel (food) that you put into your body will make it easier to burn and give you more energy. If you use improper fuel, your engine will react badly, just like in your car. Have you ever followed a car that is choking on itself and spitting out smoke? The same goes for your body. They're both machines and both need the right kind of fuel.

Eating right does not take rocket science. It is about making some sensible changes and returning to a more natural way of living.

It is about eating well and living well and thinking natural, healthy, quality taste and smaller wonderful meals. The trick is to get away from processed convenience foods and the absurd quantities. Try cooking simple, but healthy meals; they really are a strong part of enjoying life. Try eating with friends and family and make it a time to communicate with each other. Take the time to talk between bites to slow everything down. You will develop stronger and better relations with your friends and family and may realize that this is really a great part of life.

Forget canned and processed - go for fresh and local

With economic challenges and a return to simpler pleasures, this is the perfect time to refocus. Try going to the market a few times a week or even a farmers market once a week. Choose seasonal fresh vegetables; choose fish and meats that are 'free range' and the healthier choice.

Shift to essential building blocks. Simple meals mean fresh, natural ingredients. Use some organic ingredients and purchase local items in season.

Check your pantry or fridge and get rid of high fat and highly processed foods and use more fruits and vegetables.

Try mixing grains and beans together; they form a complete protein and have been a basic staple for centuries.

There is no restriction on what you eat provided you pay attention to the quantities, eating 4 to 5 smaller meals a day.

When possible, try to include healthy and fresh foods in your daily diet.

Proteins – include lean meats, poultry, fish, eggs or protein powder.

Dairy – includes milk, cheese and yogurt.

Vegetables – includes any vegetable that is green or you would eat raw. You can go heavy on the vegetables if you want more food.

Starch – includes whole grains, wild rice and potatoes (sweet is healthier).

Fat – whether you realize it or not, yes, fat is essential and necessary for healthy and balanced eating. Be sure you do not eat the wrong ones. Stick with olive oil, butter, nuts and seeds.

Use your grill all year long.

Fruit – the list for this category is endless and can help satisfy many urges for something richer and more fulfilling. It is the natural way to satisfy those cravings for something sweet and the possibilities are endless.

BANANAS

Bananas could be considered an almost perfect food. According to a number of studies, bananas could have a positive impact on the following areas:

- Energy boost
- Anemia
- Blood pressure
- Brain function
- Constipation
- Heart burn
- Nervous system

- PMS
- Weight
- Ulcers
- Stress
- Strokes

How many fruits or foods do you know of that cover this amount of ground? Even the apple does not come close.

Make bananas a regular part of your favorite foods to eat on a regular basis. Want to kick it up a notch? Occasionally add a teaspoon of peanut butter.

Tip – Try peeling bananas from the bottom instead of the top – no strings and easier.

SNACKS

A great snack to consider is pistachio nuts. First of all, about 30 pistachios are only about 100 calories; taking the time to shell them adds to the benefits. You will eat them slower and feel much more satiated. It may help lower 'bad' LDL cholesterol and has more antioxidants than a cup of green tea. Oh, and one other factor, they taste great!

I like to go to Persian markets to purchase mine in bulk, they just seem fresher and tend to taste better than the pre-packaged.

Also, then you get a chance to experiment with some interesting Persian foods. Remember variety as well as interesting and different flavors are all part of the joy of eating.

NOTE – We are not talking about calorie counting or restrictions. Think about spices and using more exotic fulfilling dishes. Think European or Asian as a source for interesting flavors. If you have traveled outside the U.S., the first thing you probably noticed is the reasonable portions that were served and consumed by the locals in other countries.

Food is about the senses... how it looks, how it smells, how it feels in your mouth and how good it tastes. Enjoying good food is about taste, not about speed; it is about enjoying the moment.

One time in France, while eating a wonderful dessert, I was told by a local that I did not eat it, I swallowed it. I thought about that and they were right. They were enjoying the burst of flavors and wonderful feeling of this dessert while I inhaled it and to top it off, they all had one serving, I ate three. Lesson learned: It is not the amount that is satisfying, but that burst of flavor; savor it and enjoy it. Let the taste linger in your mouth, sometimes food is a trip back in time and maybe it reminds you of your childhood or a special memory. Enjoy the trip.

Eat 4 to 5 smaller meals a day and never skip breakfast. Make sure to include two servings from each group and if you want more, make it more vegetables and fruit.

Rethink your plate; have 4-5 ounces of quality meat or fish, 4 ounces of legumes or whole grains and 4 ounces of vegetables. No seconds – enjoy this plate of food, eating more often takes the edge off and will help keep you from over-indulging. For dessert have fruit; use your imagination.

Did you know that it is estimated that less than 33% of the population are eating the recommended servings of fruit and vegetables a day? Select natural, nutritious food loaded with healthful amino acids, vitamins and minerals, try to eliminate overly processed foods and foods loaded with unnatural substitute products.

The solution has always been right in front of us. We have just chosen convenience and quick fixes over what has worked successfully for generations before us. Food and meals used to be a chance to get together and enjoy the moment. The meal could be simple, but the ingredients were fresh and tasty. Actually, cooking should also be part of the process, then taking the time to enjoy the meal and the company. Today, most of us live and rush through life and eat what will fill the void the quickest. Families hardly ever eat together anymore; everyone has something more important to do.

Eating well is part of the Pink Pole Balance Walking lifestyle change. Without it, you will always struggle to achieve the results you need in order to live a happy, healthy, more active life.

Besides, it has been determined through a number of studies that stress and lack of sleep will add significantly to your weight issue and many other health-related problems.

For this reason, Balance Walking focuses on having balance in one's life. There are four legs to every stool, it is important that you address each one to give you the results you expect and want. A three legged stool just will not support you as well.

SODA AND SUGAR

USDA recommendation for daily sugar consumption for a person interested in eating healthy and in moderation is only 10 teaspoons per day. Sounds simple but consider most soft drinks contain more than this in a single glass. Diet soda is another 'no-no'. Also, many foods and canned products we eat are loaded with sugar. Start reading labels.

The best approach is to forget the soda and all the drinks and foods loaded with sugars. We recommend WATER, WATER, WATER. Get a good water filter for your supply and forget all about those plastic bottles. Use a stainless or glass bottle to drink from. I like to enhance the flavor with some mint leaves and occasionally a drop of honey.

With fruit juice, I always use about ¾ of my glass filled with water and ice then top off with 100% organic fruit juice.

This gives you a sweet taste plus all the benefits of the antioxidants. I also like to use pomegranate, blueberry and cranberry. Whenever possible I also try to get organic juice. Don't forget it must be 100% juice otherwise you are getting more sugar than filler.

FOOD LABELS

Fat and calories are what most people look at when reading labels, but don't forget SODIUM.

Many packaged foods and soups are loaded with salt. Don't ignore this number; most people are eating easily 2 to 3 times the amount of sodium they should be eating.

We discussed making meals a special time to wind down and to share the moment with family or friends.

NOTE: Turn off the TV and don't ever eat while you are watching TV.

STRONGER BONES

Exercise will help but if you are aging and/or suffering from illness or treatments, you are at risk to lose bone strength and density. Eat and drink foods that naturally contain calcium, such as milk and other dairy products, yogurt and cheese. They taste good and are good for you! Eating wholesome foods are the key... not over the counter substitutes that at best are very loosely controlled. If all these substitutes and short cuts worked would we be in the shape we are in today?

Some other simple sources include legumes, tofu and dark green leafy vegetables.

Back to a life of simplicity and eating real food.

Water – Water – Water

Water is Life

Water is necessary for life and if you want to achieve control of your weight, flushing your system with water every day is a basic requirement for healthy living. The basic requirement is 8 to 10 glasses of water a day. If you are overweight you should add an additional glass for every 25 lbs. overweight you are.

Water is the body's most important nutrient, is involved in every bodily function, and makes up 70-75% of your total body weight.

I do have to mention one thing related to water. When I was young, no-one ever mentioned you had to drink water but they did mention it was important to drink milk every day. It makes you think back when water was free, this was not an issue. Now water costs more than milk and you hear a lot more about water than milk. Maybe it is just me!

Coffee, soda, wine, these liquids do not count as water intake and will not purge your system.

Want an extra cleanser for your body? Add a teaspoon of apple cider vinegar or squeeze some fresh lemon juice into a glass of water every day. There is no question this will help cleanse and flush your system. It's very simple and something that has been done for years in many countries.

Another way to help is to have a bowl of soup before your main meal or snack, something simple, chicken, vegetable, etc.

Avoid cream or thickened soup, think simple and basic. Soup is a staple in the Far East. There are good reasons to start the meal with some soup. Another approach is to just have a bowl of soup in the evening and a small salad if you need more; easily digestible, very relaxing to eat and will give you a comfortable feeling of fullness.

If you are not a water drinker now, start off by adding a extra glass to your intake over a 10 day period, and you should be able to reach a level of water intake to balance and flush your system. You will feel the difference. Unfortunately, the majority of people do not drink enough water. Can't handle water by itself? Then think of green tea, regular tea, nothing heavily sweetened. Add a small amount of various fruit juices to your water to give it a different taste.

Learn how to navigate the food label and ingredients statement. It is not just the calories. You need to understand what is in the food you are eating.

Your total body weight compared to your height establishes your risk category.

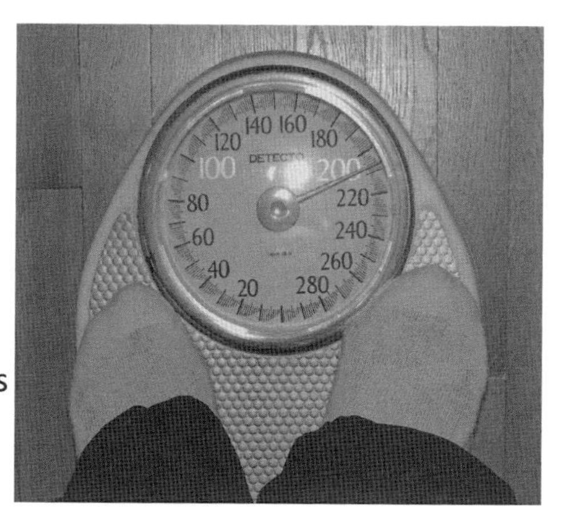

There certainly are other factors to consider and being underweight also brings risks with it too. Unfortunately, in the USA, approximately 2/3 of the population, fall into the moderate to high risk weight to height chart. This is a general calculation but the sad fact is the majority of us should be in the low risk area.

We can change this!

Note: This book is not focused on getting you to look like a movie star (but it could) or about dieting and forcing you into a self-defeating way of life. It is about reaching a level of weight and fitness that is right for you. It is about bringing balance into your life and helping you find the best way for you to enjoy your journey through life. It is about changing your lifestyle for the rest of your life with several simple steps that are very easy to accomplish. It's about living a full, active lifestyle for your complete life, not just part of it. *THIS IS ABOUT YOU!*

How would you like to improve your body and function?
I call it "active living."

Today everything is different than it was when we were children, and food just doesn't taste the same; over processed, too much sugar, picked before its time, and ripened in the back of trucks and in the market place.

Just maybe it is time to slow down our own fast paced lives and onslaught of information. We are perpetually on overload. Many countries have extended vacations yet here in the USA we are overworked with far too many working second jobs just to make ends meet.

I am not suggesting we turn back the clock but we certainly should consider slowing the pace just a little. Our children are on a free fall of information overload, processed foods and lack of physical activity. Maybe just slowing the clock down and start enjoying home cooked basic meals and reading a book instead of watching TV all night is a good start.

Return to family and basic values; please tell me it is not too late.

When I visit Europe, especially France and Italy, everything seems so different there, having simple meals even root vegetable soup loaded with garlic, fresh crusty bread and a glass of wine. It is like life and food are merged together into oneness; even the simple break for an espresso sitting at a table enjoying the moment is special.

Visit some place different every other night at the dinner table, maybe even discuss the region or country the dish originated.

You don't have to visit a foreign country. It is simple, swap recipes. There is no shortage of ways to experiment with local farmers markets. Learn to respect the mealtime experience instead of the forced chaos of the non experience most of us share today.

I don't have the time to eat right – you don't have to slave over the stove all day to eat great and to enjoy every meal.

Make all of your dishes explode with flavor by using fresh ingredients. Take any of your favorite recipes or new ones you have come across in magazines or from friends. Experiment, use fresh dark leafy greens and add fresh seasonal fruit to your salads and dishes. If you like hot, using fresh hot peppers suited to your taste will jack up the intensity of any meal. Don't want them too spicy? Take out the seeds and grill or broil in the oven. This will change the taste and take out some of the fire.

Oops, you made a mistake and it was way too hot (spicy) for you! Don't drink water! That will make it worse, go for white rice. Milk will also do the job fairly quickly.

Don't forget other simple ingredients that will add taste and crunch to your dishes. Nuts are great in salads instead of croutons, chopped chives gives you another taste. Start eating using an array of olives, nuts, seeds and flavorful oils. I am getting hungry just writing about it. Start popping edamame in your mouth for a flavorful snack instead of popcorn.

What is the deal with ORGANIC? It is showing up more and more in the food markets. Since we are trying to take a step backward where less is more and taste is what we now want, organic produce will help you reduce the trace levels of pesticides you will put in your system.

Don't go crazy, what I would recommend are the following, if you can get organic go for:

Apples, berries, nectarines, peaches, peppers, tomatoes, leafy vegetables including lettuce, spinach, arugula, celery, and root vegetables like potatoes, carrots and beets.

Those least likely to have trace levels of pesticides and you do not need organic include: Avocados, bananas, mangos, pineapple, asparagus, broccoli, eggplant, onions and cabbage.

The real secret is to cook one time for several meals, remember quantity control, it is very easy to include a few more pieces of fish or chicken even an extra vegetable.

Just changing up the mix of vegetables or using some of the chicken or fish for a salad gives you a variety with no extra work.

CHAPTER 4

TONING

Muscle mass and strength

Most people start losing muscle mass and tone after the age of thirty.

The fountain of youth and the key to feeling and looking young is muscle strength and tone. Everyone, regardless of age or physical condition, should focus on developing muscular strength, endurance, cardiovascular fitness and flexibility. The absolutely wonderful part of the body is its ability to regain muscle strength, shape and toning at any age. It is important to incorporate our recommended strength training into your Pink Pole Balance Walking program. Strength training should be done 2 to 3 times per week. This does not have to be very much time but will really help you feel good about yourself.

For toning, there are many different approaches one can take. The list will open the door to a number of simple approaches you can use. If there is an area you are familiar with or feel more comfortable with then please stay with that. Find your own comfort zone and go with it.

Yoga

I list this first because it could be very effective for toning your body and improving your flexibility.

Also, it is a cross over into your relaxation area if you want it to be.

I wonder who is smiling at whom.

This has got to be an out of body experience.

Please visit the Balance Walking website for more on Yoga positions and programs.

Resistance Bands

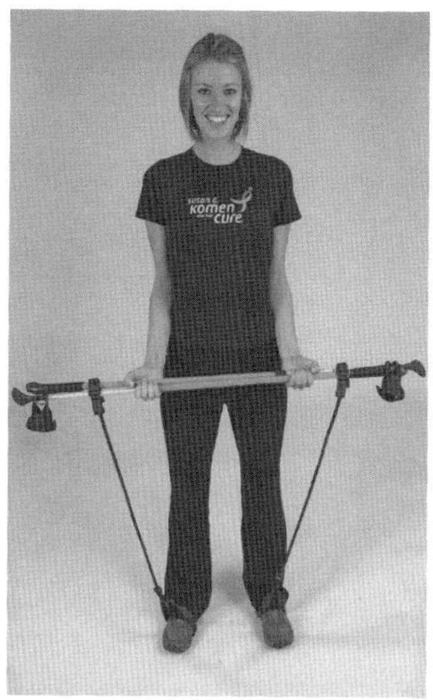

Upper Body Workout

These are like a large elastic bands, they come in different levels of resistance and are very effective for training. They are convenient and inexpensive.

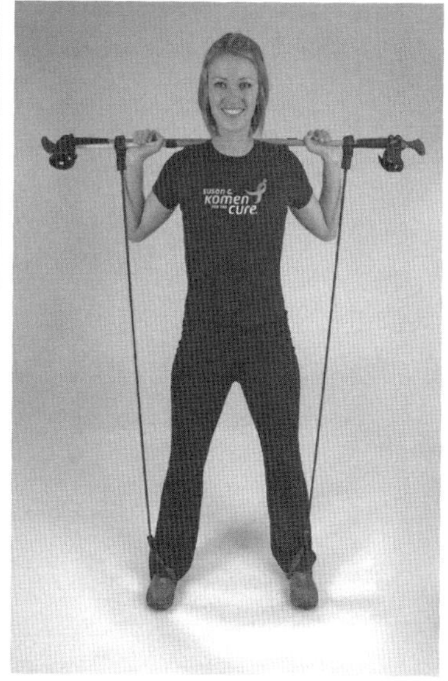

Lower Body Workout

Balance Ball

Another convenient, inexpensive way to focus on toning, this a great tool for exercise and stretching.

Pilates

Another great way to focus on toning your whole body is Pilates. Always initiating movement from your core Pilates can take you to new levels of strength and agility.

Light Weights or Kettle Bells

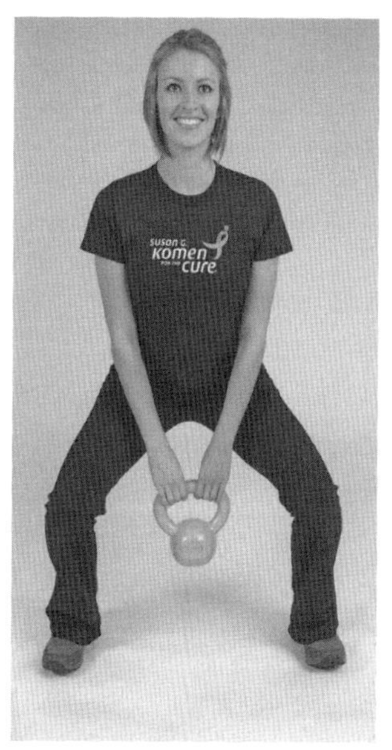

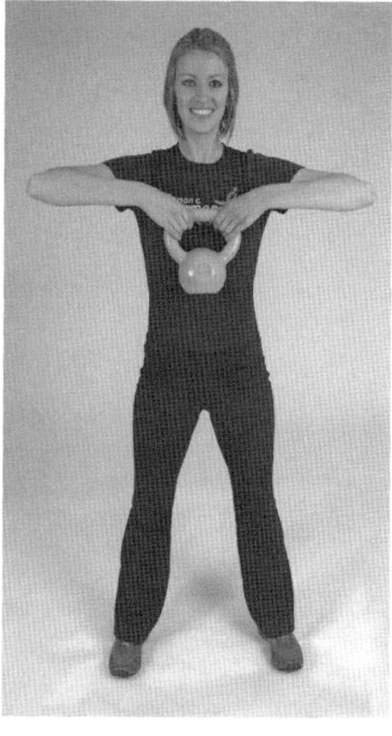

This is a good way to focus on specific areas of your body, shaping, toning and rebuilding muscle mass and strength if needed.

Basic Exercises

Obviously, this is at no cost, is very convenient, and can be done anywhere. These basic exercises and variations of them have been around forever. They include pushups, squats/step, chin ups and resistance training pitting one muscle against another.

Pick the area that you can identify with or mix them up for variety and a change of pace. This will keep you looking and feeling younger for sure.

Pink Pole Balance Walking includes all the basics needed to change your life with only the demand of 15 minutes everyday. The program goals are clear, safe, core muscle workouts that increase strength, endurance and cardiovascular performance while having fun. The result is healthy weight loss and improved muscle tone. Once again, the combination of resistance training and Pink Pole Balance Walking delivers results faster than other fitness programs.

The Balance Walking coaches and website will provide detailed information on the muscle strength and shaping routines. The key is for you to choose those that are the most suitable for your individual needs and objectives.

As an added bonus, if you use shoes specific to Balance Walking, they will increase your strength workout results providing additional challenges to your body and workout.

Other options include simple exercises, lightweight routines, resistance training, Pilates, etc. – anything that will work your muscles enough to force your body to do some rebuilding. The glorious part here is that you can mix this up; shock your muscles by hitting them from every angle. Remember we are elongating muscles as well as improving flexibility. We are creating a body for fluid movement, grace and longevity. Visit our website for suggestions and different exercises to help change up your program and keep it interesting. Check on local coaches' events and free training classes by going online at www.balancewalking.com.

Carrying extra weight increases your risk for many diseases, but for physical injuries to your feet, ankles, knees and back as well. When you walk and run you increase the impact and pressure on them. As one reaches middle age the average person will lose about one pound a year of muscle mass, usually replacing it with fat cells. Strength training will reduce your waistline and critical belly fat. The rate at which your body burns calories slows down as you age; this is another reason why eating smaller meals more often and reducing calorie intake as we age is critical for winning the battle of the bulge.

Regular exercise also serves as a detoxification method. The lymphatic system is being flushed and cells are being flooded with health giving oxygen. You can also detoxify by including a teaspoon of apple cider vinegar everyday in a glass of water, an alternative would be a teaspoon of fresh lemon juice in a glass of water. Also a slice of lemon, lime or almost any fruit will give your glass of water a new taste. This is very helpful for those having trouble drinking an abundance of water every day.

Use a sauna as a dry-heat sweat bath. Sweating helps rid the body of toxins and excess water, regulates body temperature and invigorates the body's largest organ, the skin. One thing is clear, in order to maintain balance you need to follow the complete program; one healthy behavior without the others will not work. You need to maintain all four of the Pink Pole Balance Walking program segments to change your lifestyle and maintain the desired long-term results.

Balancing Imbalance for Better Health and Fitness

Muscle Activation Specialist Teresa Tapp originally created the T-Tapp Workout as a wellness workout to improve lymphatic health, decrease back pain and build better balance but its popularity soared once people discovered how effective it was for losing inches and improving tone. Most people lose an inch off their hips or waist within a week and lose one or two clothing sizes within a month without using weights or equipment. Its special sequence of comprehensive activation of multiple muscles in combination with leverage isometrics is designed to improve body alignment and neurokinetic (mind-to-muscle) transmission so more muscles develop density, not just mass, with "spandex power" to cinch in, uplift, tighten and tone. In simple terms, T-Tapp helps your body maximize muscle movement so it can receive more benefits in less time. That's why only one set of 8 repetitions is ever needed with T-Tapp!

Tapp's focus on lymphatic function also helps your body decrease inflammation and eliminate cellular toxicity. Anti-aging expert Dr. Nicholas Perricone says "The T-Tapp System is the ideal anti-aging workout because it helps reduce inflammation, build more muscle and improve bone density." That is why T-Tapp works so well for those who have auto-immune issues like arthritis, fibromyalgia, chronic fatigue syndrome and multiple sclerosis.

In addition to being an all-in-one workout that builds heart health, bone density and muscles that are equally strong and flexible, T-Tapp is also an educational program that explains how to increase muscle activation with any type of exercise or activity.

Teresa believes that understanding how to activate your muscles and move your body to increase efficiency and effectiveness is the secret to success in building a body that looks and feels better. T-Tapp is empowering because it teaches the how and why for every exercise as well as how to fit fitness into your day...anytime, anywhere.

Teresa created the following warm up sequence to help everyone be aligned and ready to receive and achieve better brain and body fitness from balanced walking. For more information on the T-Tapp Workout you can read Teresa's book Fit and Fabulous in 15 Minutes or go to www.t-tapp.com for some FREE Try before You Buy exercises.

Teresa Tapp

Also go to the Balance Walking website to view a number of exercises Teresa created just for Balance Walking.

Ski Stretch Sequence

Align poles with your hips and slightly tilt your upper body forward. Then push your body weight into the poles to lift your ribs, arch your back and aim your tailbone up. Continue this pole pressure while you extend arms out and lower your body down to best ability without relaxing ribs, arch or tailbone. (Counts 1-4) Then push, tuck and curl your spine all the way up with head down until count 8 (Counts 5-8). Repeat for a total of 16 counts.

Form tip: push knees out more when you tilt your upper body forward and down. Also, as flexibility increases, try to lower your upper body until shoulders are level with hips (not shown in photo).

Rock-n-Roll Sequence

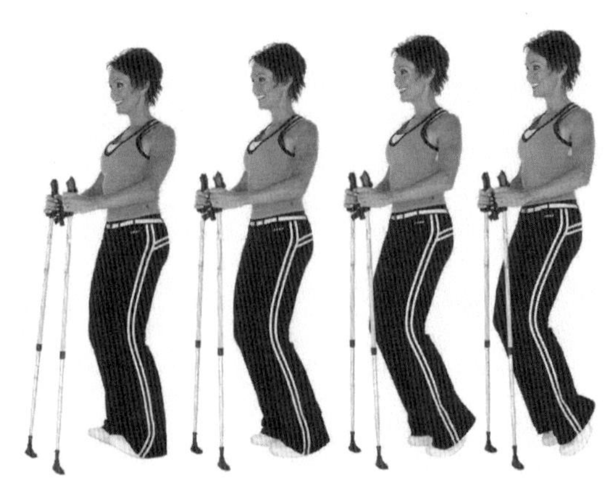

Push into your poles to lift ribs up and shift weight back onto your heels. Then continue this pressure while you roll your feet all the way up and all the way back.

Form tip: Maintain T-Tapp stance (ribs up, shoulders back, butt tucked and knees out) at all times during movement.

Push and Release Pile Squats

Starting position - Place your feet shoulder-width apart, with toes turned out at a 30-degree angle or less. Your knees should be slightly bent, your butt tucked and your knees out until you feel your arches lift. Now push poles until you feel your ribs lift and back muscles tighten.

Continue to push your knees out while you lower your body (Counts 1-3, hold 4). Then tuck your butt harder, push your knees out more and increase pole pressure as you come up against gravity (Counts 5-7, hold 8). Repeat for a total of 8 pile squats, 8 counts each.

Set Your Goals

Challenge yourself – don't forget to vary your routine, otherwise it will become just that - a boring routine leading to burn out and muscle memory retention which, in turn, will reduce the results of your program. Setting short and long-term, realistic and challenging goals will work, and changing up your routine will increase your potential success.

The retention of muscle strength and the reversing of traditional loss of muscle mass: The average person in good physical shape loses approximately 25 to 30% of their muscle mass from age 30 to 70.

It not only effects the way we feel but it adds to the slow down of the body and metabolism. Muscle mass burns more calories and keeps the fire burning. This is an area you cannot ignore. Take your clothes off and look into the mirror. Take a good look, noticing where you are sagging or starting to sag. It may not be pretty, but if you don't check this out and be honest with yourself you will never change. This is not about your high school reunion - it is about your life.

Toning and shaping will give new life to how you look and feel. Combine this firming and shaping with improved body alignment; a by product of the Chung Shi shoes and Pink Pole Balance Walking program. Your friends and family will notice the difference. You will look and feel years younger and all for a small investment of only 15 minutes per day.

Optional alternatives include Power Yoga; check out www.yoga-doc.com, the website of Dr. Craig Aaron. I have attended his classes and Dr. Aaron's version of power yoga will improve your flexibility and reshape your body. With just a couple of postures he will put your body in meltdown mode.

If you had to choose one yoga exercise then I would strongly recommend the Salutation to the SUN (Soorya Namaskar).

The Sun is considered to be the deity for health and longevity. The Sun experience will bring back lost flexibility and take you through 12 positions. You can do this in normal yoga form or be more aggressive with power yoga; the choice is yours. There are many sources and instructors available for basic yoga techniques if you are interested in this area.

CHAPTER 5

EQUIPMENT

The great thing about Balance Walking is you can start this program with a very inexpensive set of Balance Walking poles and a comfortable pair of regular walking shoes.

Our Recommendation

Poles

To start with we recommend the Susan G. Komen for the Cure® 'Pink Pole'. It is adjustable, a great starter pole, inexpensive and will also result in a $5 donation to the Susan G. Komen for the Cure® for every pair purchased.

Dressing for Balance Walking

The right shoes and socks are important and there is more information on our website. Pink Pole Balance Walking can be done in all kinds of weather but you must dress accordingly.

- Dress in layers
- Wear clothes that breathe
- Wear loose fitting clothes

You will want to dress so you are comfortable and won't get chilled. Especially when first starting to warm up or even walking or driving to your trail area.

Clothing should be comfortable and made from functional and breathable material. For the more serious Balance Walker, athletic leggings and sports tops are recommended.

A handy additional feature for your clothing is the addition of small pockets which can hold the rubber paws of your poles when they are not required. For anyone recovering from breast surgery, it is recommended that they also purchase compression arm sleeves.

Important: Once you start walking, you will get warmer. Depending on weather and conditions, as you warm up, if dressed in layers, you can take a layer off. Remember, as you slow down, and before you cool off, make sure you put your extra layer back on, this is common sense and will prevent chill.

Layering is important especially in colder weather. While Balance Walking in the winter in upstate New York, I learned very quickly that layering is critical.

In cold weather, if you are aggressively Pink Pole Balance Walking, you will warm up. When you stop or slow down the pace if you don't have a layer to put on you will chill down very rapidly. That is the great thing about Balance Walking - you can make it a very easy going pace or you can accelerate the pace, for you more competitive and fit people.

Pink Pole Balance Walking is not extreme in any way but for those of you that do push yourselves, dressing properly and taking care not to get chilled is important. Remember, Pink Pole Balance Walking is for fun and for you to enjoy yourself, to become one with nature and yourself or to enjoy the companionship of a partner or group.

Shoes

The most distinguishing feature between an ordinary fitness or running shoe and a shoe for Balance Walking is the construction of the heel and forefoot (because of the more forceful heel strike and toe off of the Balance Walking stride). If you want to become a regular Balance Walker then the acquisition of suitable footwear is highly advised. Foot Solutions carries a full line of physiological footwear such as Chung Shi Rocker and Roller bottoms.

Chung Shi Rocker Bottom Shoes

It all starts with a uniquely designed shoe that will help accelerate your program. In addition you can wear this shoe all day for your normal activity, increasing the benefits without changing your schedule.

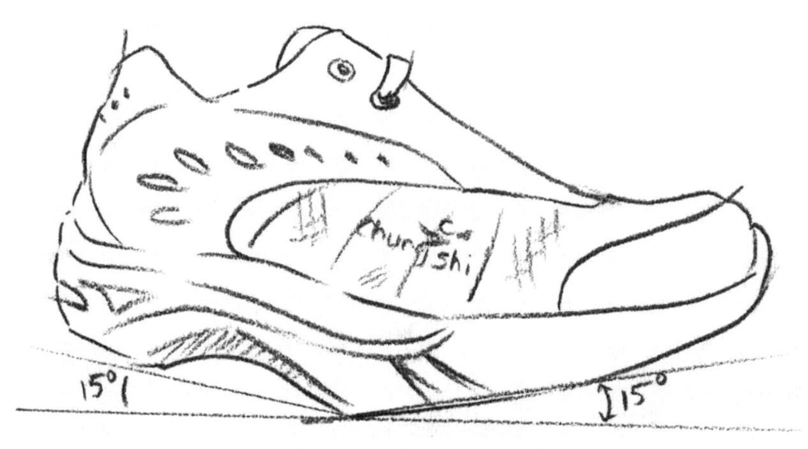

The Secret is in the Sole!

Chung Shi's unique, patented, angled sole encourages a soft heel strike with a natural, forward rolling action. Chung Shi directs the entire body to move through the proper biomechanical motion into a stable, correct gait with a shortened stride. The jarring action of walking and jogging on hard surfaces is greatly reduced.

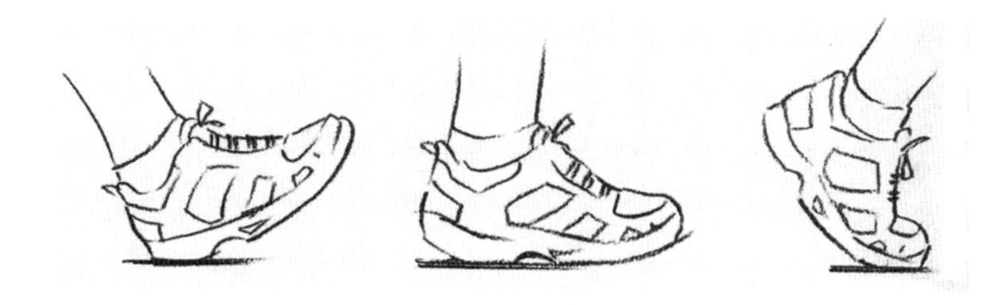

A) Angled sole aligns the body when standing and softens the heel strike, reducing jarring effect while walking or jogging.

B) The rolling ramp directs correct motion, promoting forward drive.

C) Angled sole directs a natural, propulsive rolling motion at toe-off that promotes an aligned gait.

Choose the level that's right for your body and your goals!

This is a unique innovative shoe that will move your program to a new level.

Chung Shi Comfort Step has a 15-degree angle at the heel and toe, creating a natural rolling motion that is perfect for standing, walking and jogging.

Chung Shi Balance Step takes your workout to an entirely new level. It features a 20-degree angle at the heel and toe and has a higher apex at the rolling ramp. This forces muscles to work much harder than Comfort Step. It is the most aggressive alignment and muscle-use shoe available.

Do not be fooled by the similar looking shoes in the market. You will feel the difference when you slip your feet into Chung Shi's and you will be challenged.

Testimonial from Teresa Tapp who has been using Chung Shi in her workouts and classes since 2006:

I LOVE Chung Shi shoes! From the very first time I tried them on in 2006, I've never found another shoe that does so much for my body inside and out. As a muscle activation specialist and creator of an award winning fitness program, I understand how important mindful movement and body alignment are for better health and fitness. Not only do my Chung Shi shoes help me stay pain free, their one of a kind design helps keep my body fit and firm.

Teresa Tapp – author of Fit and Fabulous in 15 minutes and creator of *T-Tapp, The Workout that Works* at www.t-tapp.com.

Socks

We discussed properly fitted shoes and how important it is to have the right size and shaped shoe.

For Balance Walking my sock of choice is Padds by Thorlo.

This sock is designed to cushion the fatty pad areas on the bottom of your feet that get worn out and displaced as we age and exercise. Socks are a major part of an integrated solution for your individual feet, along with shoes and properly designed arch supports. Some people are concerned about the thickness of socks or pads making their feet too hot. Usually, the feeling of hot or cold feet is caused by improper fitting shoes and/or socks. This is why I mention the integrated product system solution.

The proper thickness of the sock and properly fitted shoes allows a more complete range of motion of the feet, at the same time protecting against friction and chafing from the inside of the shoe.

This approach helps to stimulate circulation in the feet while the sock helps provide insulation and air flow, which helps moderate temperature and keeps the feet from getting too hot or too cold. Make socks part of your complete exercise package.

Compression Sleeves

When you need help managing lymphedema you should consider using compression sleeves when exercising or Balance Walking. As always check with your therapist or doctor first.

Compression sleeves are available in different colors and compression levels.

This is very similar to a compression sock but designed for your arms.

There are a number of websites that you can research for compression sleeves.

A wide range of these sleeves can be found at www. lymphedivas.com, this is one of the several sites I visited that you may want to check out.

REFERENCES

Balance Pole Walking burns up to 46% more calories than exercise walking without poles or moderate jogging. (Cooper Institute, 2004, Dallas and other). Extremely great weight loss program in combination with conscious nutrition. Note: this study does not include our Balance Walking rocker bottom shoes which will increase burn rate.

Increases heart and cardiovascular training to 22% more effect (Foley 1994, Jordan 2001, Morss t al., 2001 and other).

Incorporates 90% of all body muscles in one exercise and increases endurance of arm muscles (triceps) and neck and shoulder muscles (Latissmus) to 38% (Karawan et al., 1992 and other).

Eliminates back, shoulder and neck pain (Attila et al., 1999 and other).

Less impact on hip, knee and foot joints about 26% (Wilson et al., 2001 and other).

Increase production of “positive” hormones. Decreases “negative” hormones (R.M. Klatz et. Al., 1999; Dharma Singh Khalsa 1997).

Supports stress management and mental disorders (Stoughton 1992, Momment-Jauch, 2003).

Human Performance Laboratory, University of Calgary, Bio-Mechanics of walking in the Chung Shi health shoe, October, 2006.

National Consumer Research 2005, Finland. Research article on Nordic pole walking and health benefits new German fitness trend makes strides 2005.

Research on results on responses to pole walking training published in 1992 by Stoughton, Sarken and Kareven from the University of Oregon.

Effect of Chung Shi walking shoes on posture, foot shape, balance, flexibility, menstruation, pain, body composition, and gait, EWHA Women's University, Gait Biomechanics Laboratory, Yi Kyung OK, November, 2006.

CDC (Centers for Disease Control and Prevention) - April 2005.

Studies show that African American women are more likely to gain weight at diagnosis which may increase their risk to cancer reoccurrence as well as their mortality rate. Physical activity has been shown to decrease body mass index and improve quality of life in cancer survivors.

I am not saying anything new here there are plenty of studies that validate these findings. So the objective here is to change your attitude and get you started on a Pink Pole Balance Walking program.

Pole Walking – Standing Exercise
www.breastcancer.about.com - October 28, 2009
The Effect of Walking Poles on Shoulder Function in Breast Cancer Survivors
ict.sagepub.com/content/abstract/4/4/287

Nordic Walking is welcoming the Balance Walking Method
PR-USA.net - April 7, 2009

Study finds women exercise less after breast cancer diagnosis.
American Cancer Society 2003/04/18

Lymphedema and Exercise
www.lymphedema-therapy.com

Weight Lifting Benefit in Breast Cancer Survivors
Cnn.com - October 21, 2009

Exercise Boosts Well-Being after Breast Cancer
Medline Plus - October 1, 2009

Is the whole larger than the sum of the parts? The promise of combining physical activity and diet to improve cancer outcomes
Journal of Clinical Oncology – June 10, 2007

Diet and Exercise Key to Surviving Breast Cancer, Regardless of Obesity, New UCSD study says.
Medical News Today – June 13, 2007

Intensity and Timing of Physical Activity in Relation to Post Menopause Breast Cancer Risk: The Prospective NIH-AARP Diet and Health Study.
BMC Cancer 2009, 9:349

Younger Next Year for Women – Chris Crowley & Henry S. Lodge, M.D

Chris and Henry have a great approach to aging or should I say anti-aging. I read 'Younger Next Year for Men' and really enjoyed it. I picked up 'Younger Next year for Women' for my wife and she enjoyed it.

The bottom line is it is never too late too reverse the aging process, the body will react positively to very simple changes.

I believe it is another reference tool and reinforcement on the changes you must start making now if you want to turn the clock back.

Kimberly Hard, Author of *Introduction to Yoga*
Provided information and poses from her book
www.bewellatlanta.com

Breast Cancer News

4/14/09 updated Table 57: Physical activity and breast cancer survival

http://www.komen.org/physicalactivityresearch

Walking Specific

5/31/2005 Breast Cancer Patients Could Reap Big Rewards from Walking

http://www.komen.org/walkingrewards

Risk Etc

Understanding Risk

http://www.komen.org/BreastCancer/UnderstandingRisk.html

About the Author

Ray Margiano, PhD and Pedorthist, is the Founder & CEO of Foot Solutions, Inc., and the visionary innovator who created the Balance Walking program for health, wellness, fitness and prevention. He is a true entrepreneur and has started and managed several successful companies. He is a tireless innovator who loves what he does and loves to give back.

Ray serves on the American Diabetes Association's Advisory Board, is a member of the Board of Governors at the University of New Haven, is on the Board of Directors for the National Shoe Retailers Association, is a Visionary Board Member for the International Council on Active Aging and is on the Kennesaw State University's WellStar College of Health and Human Services Advancement Board.

Ray is actively involved in many outreach programs besides the Balance Walking groups for breast cancer which is focused on wellness and prevention; there is the children's obesity program, diabetes, the Presidents Challenge program for getting Americans back in shape... retirement community programs and international programs such as the 'Blue Planet Run' for pure drinking water. Ray is an active participant of 'Soles for Souls', donating shoes for flood, fire and the needy and is also involved on a national basis in Breast Cancer walks, Diabetic, Arthritic, Heart walks and Get Out Get Active campaign to promote healthier living.

Ray's philosophy is that it is easier to do preventative maintenance than to fix it after it is broken. Balance Walking focuses on lifestyle changes to work on prevention, wellness and living fuller happier lives.

Ray Margiano has a BS from the University of New Haven, an MS from Rensselaer Polytechnic Institute and a PhD from Canbourne University.

Ray is a mentor, an entrepreneur & author.

Ray introduced Balance Walking in 2008 with his first book.